TT:ISLE OF MAN
RIDER BY RIDER

TT-ISLE OF MAN
RIDER BY RIDER

First published in the UK in 2013

© Demand Media Limited 2013

www.demand-media.co.uk

Printed and bound in China.

ISBN 978-1-909217-77-5

The views in this book are those of the author but they are general views only and readers are urged to consult the relevant and qualified specialist for individual advice in particular situations. Demand Media Limited hereby exclude all liability to the extent permitted by law of any errors or omissions in this book and for any loss, damage or expense (whether direct or indirect) suffered by a third party relying on any information contained in this book.

CONTENTS

Introduction

The riders who compete in the Isle of Man Tourist Trophy are amongst the bravest and well-known sports people on the planet, and they along with countless fans flock to the small island in the Irish Sea every May and June.

The greatest motorcycle race in the world may be based on the Isle of Man but its origins can be traced across the Atlantic Ocean to New York and James Gordon Bennett who was born in 1841 to a wealthy American publisher and founder of the New York Herald. Bennett was brought up in a world of luxury, although he did serve in the navy during the American Civil War before taking over his father's business at 26.

Keen to raise the profile of the Herald, Bennett funded Henry Stanley's successful expedition to search for Dr David Livingstone in Africa. It seemed as if Bennett could do no wrong but then he committed a social faux pas while intoxicated at a party in 1877 and his engagement to Caroline May was called

off. He left the United States to settle in France and spent time on his yacht, the Lysistrata, and at a villa on the Cote d'Azur.

Bennett continued managing his publishing empire and established the Paris Herald in 1887. He then developed a fascination with the newly invented motorcar and decided to hold an international race, the Gordon Bennett Challenge Cup, in 1899. The rules were simple: a nation was allowed to enter three cars (with a maximum weight of a ton each) that had to be raced by drivers affiliated to their country's national club over a 352-mile course.

The inaugural Gordon Bennett race took place on June 14th 1900 between Paris and Lyon. Teams from France, Belgium and Germany entered but poor organisation led to many of the competitors getting lost. The following year, the ACF (Automobile Club de France) ran the event alongside the existing Paris-Bordeaux race.

A notable foreign entry competed

in 1901 in the shape of Australian entrepreneur Selwyn Francis Edge at the wheel of an English 50-horsepower Napier. Edge's tyres performed so poorly, however, that he was forced to fit French rubber halfway through and was disqualified. Edge's troubles were typical of the time as both the car and motor-racing as a sport were still in their infancy.

At the turn of the 20th century, the Locomotive Amendment Act of 1865 (the Red Flag Act) required all self-propelled vehicles to be preceded by a flag-carrying pedestrian to warn oncoming traffic. Speeds were limited to 4 mph on highways and 2 mph in towns and villages. Matters improved in 1896 with the introduction of the Locomotives & Highways Act that allowed vehicles of less than three tons to travel at up to 12 mph and this was then increased to 20 mph in 1903 under the Motor-Car Act. These restrictions, coupled with an Act of Parliament prohibiting racing on public roads,

Above: *Selwyn Francis Edge at the wheel*

stifled vehicle development in the UK and allowed the foreign manufacturers to open up a big technological lead as their machines were now capable of 60 mph.

The 1902 Gordon Bennett Challenge Cup from Paris to Innsbruck was run in conjunction with the popular Paris-Vienna road race. Of the 219 entrants only six were from France and Britain. The British seemed doomed to fail before the start as the Wolseleys of Arthur Callan and Claude Grahame-White arrived five hours late and were plagued with problems. Edge was having another go in an improved Napier but he only just made it to the start in time having been forced to change his gearbox.

The Wolseleys retired and French drivers Girardot and Fournier suffered a split fuel tank and broken clutch respectively. Only Edge's Napier and the Panhard of Frenchman René De Knyff remained in contention as the race swept through Basel and Zurich and on to the Austrian border at Bregenz. Only the 1800-metre Arlberg Pass now stood in their way. Both drivers fought hard on the ascent but De Knyff's Panhard had earlier suffered a broken differential sleeve and he retired at the top of the pass. Edge raced on to Innsbruck and victory, and his unexpected win would eventually lay the foundations for the Isle of Man TT.

The Gordon Bennett Challenge Cup regulations stated that the club of the winning nation would host the following year's competition. However, Britain's draconian speed limits and ban on public-road-racing meant it was impossible for Britain to comply. It was then pointed out that the Automobile Club of Great Britain also included Ireland, which, as it quickly passed the Light Locomotives (Ireland) Bill allowing racing on public roads, could host the event and promote tourism.

A course was chosen around the town of Athy in County Kildare. A 40-mile loop would be raced three times and a 52-mile loop four times. The Irish embraced the idea and the 327-mile race grew into a two-week festival with many support events. Four nations entered the 1903 race – Great Britain, France, Germany and the USA – but despite showing well in the early laps Edge had tyre issues and slipped behind the continental drivers. Victory eventually went to Belgian ace Camille Jenatzy driving a Mercedes for the Germans.

The fledgling British motor industry finally realised that auto racing was the perfect platform from which to promote its machinery but it needed a venue for an exciting circuit that would lure the Europeans to Britain and would test man and machine equally. Julian Orde, Secretary of the Automobile Club of Great Britain & Ireland, became

convinced that the Isle of Man could host the race so he set off in his Wolseley in 1904 to discuss the idea with the Governor of the Isle of Man, who just happened to be the Right Honourable George Fitzroy Henry Somerset (Orde's cousin). The people of the island enthusiastically supported the idea because they believed the Isle of Man warranted a place on the international map.

A bill was proposed to the Tynwald and passed with little amendment. Then King Edward VII gave his permission and the first trials took place on May 10, 1904. To the delight of the islanders, five Napiers, three Wolseleys and three Weir-Darracqs contested five 51-mile laps of a course that started at Quarter Bridge in Douglas before heading south through Ballasalla and Castletown and then swinging north through Foxdale and Glen Helen to Ballaugh and onto Sandygate. The cars then raced east to the streets of Ramsey before joining the New Mountain Road back to Douglas and Quarter Bridge.

Clifford Earp in a Napier recorded the fastest time of 7 hours 26 minutes. The following day he came second to Selwyn Edge in a hill-climb from

Above: *Rene de Knyff in his Panhard in 1899*

to the southwest of Paris with teams from Austria, Denmark, France, Germany and Great Britain taking part. Victory went to Frenchman M Demster but the British finished well down the field. The race provoked a barrage of criticism about the organization and conditions so the entrants decided to found the Fédération Internationale des Clubs Motocyclistes (FICM), the forerunner of motorcycle racing's current governing body, the Fédération Internationale de Motocyclisme (FIM).

Before the 1905 International Cup the British motorcycle club held selection trials to improve the team's chances. The Isle of Man seemed the ideal proving ground and the trials were arranged for the day after the cars had completed their events. The motorcycles were scheduled to compete over the same course but the cars had carved the roads up and a revised route ran south from Quarter Bridge to Castletown and then north to St John's before heading east and back to Quarter Bridge.

Eighteen riders entered the inaugural International Motorcycle Cup Race on the Isle of Man's 25-mile course but seven either didn't make it through scrutineering or failed to make the

Lewaigue near Ramsey to Maughold Church. On the third day, speed trials over a measured kilometre were held on Douglas's Promenade. Edge won the trial but he lost control and collided with a wall while returning from his fastest run and sustained serious injuries. Despite this, the trials were deemed a success and Edge was selected to represent the United Kingdom in the 1904 Gordon Bennett Challenge Cup.

Later that year a new race for motorcycles was introduced. The International Cup was held in Dourdan

start line due to a mixture of technical infringements, breakdowns and crashes. Finally, at 3.30 am on May 31st 1905, W.H. Hodgkinson set out from Quarter Bridge and became the first person to ride a motorcycle competitively on the Isle of Man. The legend had been born. The race over five laps was won by J.S. Campbell on an Ariel at an average of 30 mph despite his machine briefly catching fire during a pit-stop.

The 1906 event was held in Austria but it was marred by accusations of cheating. Secretary of the Auto-Cycle Club Freddie Straight and the Collier brothers (Charlie and Harry), representing Matchless motorcycles, suggested permanently basing the bike event on the automobile races that were already being held on the Isle of Man. At a meeting of the club in London in January 1907 the idea was proposed and two touring classes were suggested: single-cylinder machines averaging 90 mpg and twins averaging 75 mpg. The motorcycles had to be fitted with saddles, pedals, mudguards and silencers to emphasise the touring nature of the event.

The first official TT was expected to pit the single-cylinder Triumphs of

Above: Oliver Godfey at the 1911 TT

Hulbert and Jack Marshall against the Collier brothers on their Matchless machines. After 158 miles, Charlie Collier was declared the winner with a time of 4 hours 8 minutes and 8 seconds. Marshall and Hulbert joined him on the podium. In the twin-cylinder class, Rembrandt Fowler brought his Norton home in 4 hours 21 minutes and 53 seconds, just ahead of W.H. Wells on a Vindec and W.M. Heaton on a Rex.

In 1908, 36 riders entered but the motorcycles had their pedals removed (to ensure a win was down to pure

Right: *The Norton Twin of Rembrandt Fowler who won the first official TT in 1907*

mechanical power and not rider-assisted) and marshals were sworn in as special constables to keep the course free from spectators and other traffic after concerns were raised over safety. Harry Reid took the twin win, while Marshall ousted Collier in the single class.

The following year the rules were changed slightly so that the singles were allowed up to 500cc and the twins 750cc, but there would only be one title up for grabs as the classes had effectively been combined. Harry Collier won the trial and was then second to brother Charlie in 1910. Speeds and reliability gradually

improved and Harry Bowen raised the lap record to over 50 mph on his BAT twin but he then crashed into wooden safety boards on the bend at Ballacraine.

In 1911 the riders had to negotiate the full mountain circuit. One hundred and four men lined up at the start, including Charlie Collier and Rem Fowler. The Junior TT for 300cc singles and 340cc twins attracted 35 entrants and was won by Percy Evans on a Humber at 41.45 mph. The Senior Race for 500cc singles and 580cc twins over five laps of the 37.5-mile Snaefell Mountain Course ended up in a 1-2 for the Indians of

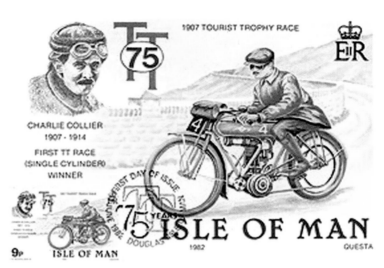

Oliver Godfrey and Charles Franklin at nearly 48 mph.

There were constant amendments to the rules and safety measures, such as the compulsory wearing of crash helmets, but that didn't prevent Frank Walker being killed after he crashed into a wooden barrier after the finish line. Motorcycle sales, on the other hand, were booming and factory bikes benefited hugely from the advances made by the racing teams.

One hundred and forty-seven riders, many of them wealthy privateers, entered in 1913. Tim Wood won the Senior TT despite having to spend ten minutes in the pits repairing an oil leak. The start was moved to the top of Bray Hill the following year so that the size of the paddock could be increased and the view for spectators improved.

Oliver Godfrey was one of the early TT pioneers who didn't return from the battlefields on the continent at the end of the war, and racing didn't resume until 1920, two years after hostilities ceased. There was now a Lightweight class and the course had been lengthened slightly to 37.73 miles. In 1925 Wal Handley became the first man to win two races in a week when he took the Junior TT and Ultra-Lightweight race for Rex-Acme. The Senior TT was won by Howard Davis on his own bike despite stiff competition from the works teams with the bigger budgets and full-time mechanics.

Above: *A stamp commemorating Charlie Collier's TT win in 1907*

Left: *Wal Handley takes the right-hander at Creg-ny-Baa in the 1926 TT*

Above: *A signed Percy Hunt photo after his historic 1931 double on a Norton*

Safety issues were again raised after several pit fires involving alcohol-based fuels, so the organisers limited the teams to conventional petrol. The road surfaces had been sand and gravel but they were tarmac by the end of the decade. The roads were completely closed during the racing after Archie Birkin, brother of world-famous Bentley Boy Tim, was killed on the corner at Kirk Michael (it was later renamed Birkin's Bend). More fatalities threatened the event's future and forced the organisers to widen the A18 mountain road and remove the humpback bridge at Ballig. The TT was now so popular that manufacturers used the event to showcase the latest innovations in bike technology and safety. The technical advances included supercharging, overhead camshafts, rear suspension and telescopic forks, and average speeds increased rapidly. As top speeds were now approaching three figures, better handling was the best way to lower lap times.

In the 1930s the TT became the major motorcycling event on the calendar, and indeed many see this as the golden age of

Left: *Stanley Woods in the Senior TT on a Moto Guzzi at the Isle of Man in 1935*

bike racing on the island. Wal Handley became the first rider to win all three main classes and lap the mountain course in less than half an hour. Manufacturers Rudge and Norton battled it out for supremacy, and in 1931 Percy Hunt scored a Senior/Junior double. Average lap speeds were now over 80 mph so accidents were far more serious. Indeed Wal Handley was forced to retire after coming off at the 11th milestone in 1932. The decade was dominated by Stanley Woods, Jimmy Simpson (who was the first to lap the famous circuit at 60, 70 and 80 mph), Tim Hunt and Jimmy Guthrie, although the latter was killed at the 1937 German Grand Prix. Murray Walker's father, Graham, scored five podium finishes, including one in the sidecar TT in 1923, before winning the 1931 Lightweight TT on a Rudge.

Norton pulled out of the event in 1939 as they were moving to a war footing. The first overseas winner of the main event, the Senior TT, was German Georg 'Schorsch' Meier in 1939. As was customary, he was allowed to keep the trophy for a year but Europe descended

Right: *Jacques Drion and Inge Stoll-Laforge at the TT in 1954*

Far Right: *The peerless Geoff Duke on a Manx Norton*

into war and the TT was cancelled for six years. The trophy was eventually found in a shop in Vienna in 1945.

Bike racing returned to the Isle of Man in 1946 with the Manx Grand Prix, but the TT had to wait another year. Low-quality petrol meant that speeds were well down on the pre-war averages and they were further lowered by banning supercharging. A number of different clubmans classes were introduced, however, and more fans than ever flocked to the island. Over the next decade the course was upgraded, sidecar events were reintroduced and the first woman, Inge Stoll, entered a race. The decade was also noted for the decline in the dominance of British machines. Norton, AJS, BSA, Matchless and many other manufacturers were struggling financially and the European giants like CZ, Ducati and MV Agusta became the top marques in road racing. British riders like Geoff Duke, Bob McIntyre and John Surtees were lured to the foreign marques and had soon

Far Right: *Gilberto Parlotti's death resulted in the TT being stripped of its World Championship status*

raised the lap record to over 100 mph. By now Graham Walker had taken up a position in the commentary box and he had the privilege of calling Duke, Artie Bell and Johnny Lockett home in a historic 1–2–3 for Norton in the 1950 Senior TT. Duke, Lockett and Jack Brett also registered a 1–2–3 for Norton in the 1951 Junior TT. By 1955, however,

Norton had been replaced at the top of the leader-board by Duke's Gilera in the Senior TT, Bill Lomas's Moto Guzzi in the 350cc and his MV Agusta in the 250cc class.

The course was again modified for safety reasons in the 1960s and more new classes, such as the Ultra-Lightweight 50cc, were introduced.

A young British rider called Mike Hailwood would dominate the event for the next decade. This was the era of the Japanese manufacturers, however, and Honda stunned the establishment by taking the first five places in the 125cc and 250cc TTs in 1961. At the end of the decade Production classes were introduced which meant the racing was more accessible to everyday riders and allowed manufacturers like Triumph, Norton and BSA to return to the island and compete with the Japanese on a level playing field.

Having just enjoyed a glorious era, however, TT racing was about to be stripped of its World Championship status. From 1949 the island had been home to the British Grand Prix and a round of the World Championship but higher speeds and falling safety standards led to many deaths (seven riders were killed on the course in 1970). When Italian Gilberto Parlotti was killed in poor conditions on the mountain in 1972, ten-time TT winner, reigning champion and motorcycle Grand Prix legend Giacomo Agostini refused to race at the event. He maintained that every rider had a choice whether or not to compete, but that he wouldn't be

appearing. Spectator numbers and the quality of the racing in the following TTs were still high but four years later enough riders had joined the boycott for the event to be stripped of its status. The Grand Prix was moved to Silverstone instead.

The TT became something of a sideshow for a few years but the emergence of Irishman Joey Dunlop brought renewed interest in the spectacle and Geoff Duke's fears that the event may not have a future were thankfully unfounded. Indeed, the TT has probably benefited from becoming a one-off winner-takes-all festival and the kudos associated with winning on the island is at an all-time high. Between 1977 and 2000 the incomparable Dunlop won 26 TTs in various categories and crowds flocked to the mountain course to see him race at speeds of up to 170 mph.

Mike Hailwood made an emotional return to the island in 1978 after an 11-year hiatus. He wasn't expected to challenge Phil Read for the top honours and he gave away an early lead. But Hailwood then eased into the race and began lowering his lap times. He soon had Read in his sights and eventually passed him. The Formula One Ducati

Left: *Mick Grant*

Far Left: *Joey Dunlop at Bray Hill in 1992*

held up to the full-throttle blitz and Hailwood climbed to the top step of the podium for the first time since he'd beaten Giacomo Agostini 1967. The deaths of Mac Hobson, Kenny Birch and Ernst Trachsel, and serious head injuries to American Pat Hennen who struck a kerb at 150 mph, cast a shadow over the event, however.

Hailwood was back in 1979 but he had to withstand a tremendous challenge from an injured Mick Grant. It would be his 14th and last win on the island, and he iced the cake with a 114 mph lap record. Grant took victory in the 1980 Formula One race as some consolation, however. He would then have to contend with the genius of Joey Dunlop but the Irishman set a new lap record at 115 mph and took the Classic TT. The sidecars saw Jock Taylor and Trevor Ireson battling for the spoils. Taylor was tragically killed two years later when a second sidecar crashed into his while marshals were trying to

TT RIDER BY RIDER

Left: *Steve Hislop on a Norton at Creg-ny-Baa in 1992*

Far Left: *Ian Hutchinson would claim a record five wins at the 2010 TT*

extricate him after his accident at Imatra in Finland.

Dunlop dominated the racing throughout the decade and won six Formula One TTs, three Senior TTs, two Juniors and a Classic TT. He was equally prolific in the 1990s, taking five Ultra-Lightweight, five Lightweight, one Junior, one Formula One and a final Senior TT. Indeed only Steve Hislop with 11 victories between 1984 and 1994, Phillip McCallen also with 11 between 1989 and 1999, Ian Lougher with 10 wins since 1984, and John McGuinness with 19 since 1996 come close to the Irishman's incredible achievements at the TT in the modern era.

But the island couldn't escape its dark side. Phil Mellor, Steve Henshaw and Colin Keith were three of the eight riders who lost their lives on the course during the TT and Manx Grand Prix in 1989. Although rider safety has improved recently, 15 riders have been

Above: *John McGuinness rounds Parliament Square in the 2010 TT*

Centre: *Phil McCallen at the Gooseneck in 1992*

killed at the TT in the last decade. It's doubtful that fatalities on the course will ever be eradicated when riders will always be prone to making mistakes, and mechanical failures are an accepted hazard of bike racing. Now that the top speeds are exceeding 200 mph, any such mistakes or failures are likely to have serious consequences. The riders know and accept the dangers, however, and they all have the choice as to whether or not they should compete.

In 1996 Phillip McCallen set a new record by winning four races – the Formula One TT, Junior TT, Production TT and Senior TT – in a single week. He almost made it a clean sweep of all five races he entered but could only manage fourth in the Lightweight TT behind

Above: *Dave Molyneux and passenger Patrick Farrance on the way to Dave's 15th TT win in 2012*

Dunlop, Jim Moodie and Manxman Jason Griffiths. His record was eventually broken by Ian Hutchinson in 2010 who managed five solo wins. The outright sidecar record fell in the same period to Dave Molyneux who notched up 16 wins between 1989 and 2012.

In 2007 John McGuinness lowered the lap record for the 37.73-mile course to 17 minutes 21.99 seconds, thus becoming the first man to average more than 130 mph on a course with 250 bends and elevation changes of more than a thousand feet. Indeed Geoff Duke calls it the greatest challenge in motorsport.

Since 1907, countless riders have braved many variants of the circuit, but 50 have stood head and shoulders above their contemporaries.

Agostini

Giacomo Agostini developed a fascination for motorcycles at an early age but his father did not approve of his career so he had to slip away to compete in hill-climbs and the odd road-racing event. In 1963 Agostini won the Italian 175cc Championship on a Morini, and the following year he won the 350cc title and further proved his credentials by finishing fourth at the Italian Grand Prix at Monza.

It was impossible to keep such a talent from the bigger teams and Domenico Agusta signed Agostini to ride alongside Britain's Mike Hailwood. It was a partnership that would only last a year because Hailwood then joined Honda but it gave rise to one of the sport's great rivalries. Agostini almost won the 350cc world title at his first attempt but his bike failed him at the last round of the championship in Suzuka, handing the title to Honda's Jim Redman.

With Hailwood gone, Agostini rose to the challenge of leading the team and won the 500cc world title seven times in succession, a feat he repeated with the smaller 350cc bike. It is testament to his ability that of the 142 350cc and 500cc World Championship races he started between 1967 and 1974, he won 106 and came second in 12. If you factor in 19 retirements after crashes or mechanical failures, there were only five races in an eight-year period where he finished outside the top two, one of the greatest winning streaks in any sport.

His epic duel with Hailwood in the 1967 season saw each rider claim five wins, although Agostini clinched the title at the last race. He was totally dominant for the next five years and took his first win at the Junior TT in 1966. He then completed historic Senior/Junior doubles in 1968, 1969, 1970 and 1972, and his duel with Hailwood in the Diamond Jubilee TT saw both men repeatedly smash the lap record. To register 10 wins from just 16 TT starts shows what a consummate professional and fearless rider he must have been, but he then dropped a bombshell when he announced that he would no longer race

at motorcycling's most prestigious event because of safety concerns after the death of his friend, Gilberto Parlotti, on the course in 1972. Over the next four years – and with riders continuing to die – more riders joined the boycott and in 1977 the TT lost its status as a Grand Prix event.

Agostini then switched from MV Agusta to Yamaha and immediately won the Daytona 200. He won that year's 350cc title but injuries and breakdowns meant he couldn't double up with the 500cc title too, although he did finally claim the title, his last, in 1975. He bowed out on a high by riding a 500cc MV Agusta to victory at the Nürburgring in 1976. He retired from competitive riding the following year and tried his luck in a Formula One car. He had little success and returned to bike racing as the manager of the Marlboro Yamaha team in 1982. Under his tutelage, riders like Kenny Roberts and Eddie Lawson found their feet in the sport.

Name: Giacomo Agostini
Born: June 16th 1942, Brescia, Italy
TT Career: 1965 – 1972
TT Wins: 10

Amm

Right: *Ray Amm takes to the air on the Norton Kneeler on the Snaefell Mountain Course in 1954*

Ray Amm was a motor trader who started racing on grass tracks aged 17 on an AJS he'd bought at the end of the war. He finished last in his first race so he traded the AJS for a Triumph and then a new Norton, which allowed him to enter the 1949 Port Elizabeth 200 in South Africa. He broke the lap record and looked to be heading for victory when his clutch failed. He won the same event in the 500cc class the following year at a record average speed of 95.86 mph, and, having won for a second time in 1951, decided to move to Europe.

Amm ordered two Manx Nortons in time for the Isle of Man TT but they were late arriving so he borrowed an AJS and won the 350cc ARA meeting. He finished ninth on the Norton in the Junior TT at 81.59 mph but he was well down the field in the Senior TT. He returned in 1952 but crashed at Braddan Bridge in the Junior Race. He recovered to finish a creditable third behind the Norton of Reg Armstrong and the MV Agusta of Leslie Graham in the Senior TT, however.

Amm signed to race for the works Norton team for the remainder of 1952 but he played second fiddle to the legendary Geoff Duke, although he did win the 350cc Nations Grand Prix in Italy at the end of the season. The following year he raced the controversial streamliner, the Norton Kneeler, which had the nicknames the 'Amm Sandwich' or 'Silver Fish', but he reverted back to the original factory bike for the 1953 TT. This was an inspired choice because he won the Junior TT at 90.52 mph and then the Senior TT at 93.85 mph to record a classic double. He later fell and broke a collarbone at the French Grand Prix which ended his world

title challenge but he then set a world hour record of 133.70 miles on the Kneeler.

The 1954 Junior TT ended in disappointment when he retired from the lead but the Senior TT gave him his third and final win on the island, albeit in controversial circumstances. Duke led after the first lap by 14 seconds but Amm rode a death-defying second lap to close the gap to just two seconds. Heavy rain and low cloud shrouded the mountain and Duke decided to come into the pits to refuel. Sensing the race might be stopped, Amm refused to pit and opened up a 30-second lead. With visibility down to 20 yards, the race was stopped before Amm needed to refuel and he won at an average speed of 88.12 mph. He would later finish runner-up to Duke in the 500cc World Championship and Fergus Anderson in the 350cc series.

Amm declined several lucrative offers from other teams and joined MV Agusta in 1955. He made his debut at Imola but he lost control and crashed in poor conditions at Rivazza and died on the way to hospital.

Name: William Raymond 'Ray' Amm
Born: December 10th 1927, Salisbury, Rhodesia
Died: April 11th 1955, Imola, Italy
TT Career: 1951 - 1955
TT Wins: 3

Anstey

Bruce Anstey initially rode for Relentless Suzuki but now competes for Padgett's Honda. He made his road-racing debut at the Isle of Man in 1999 but he had to wait until 2000 for his first podium – he finished second on a DTR Yamaha TZ250 behind the great Joey Dunlop in the Lightwight TT over three laps. He eventually won the same race in 2002, finishing three minutes ahead of Simon Smith.

In 2003 Anstey gave Triumph its first TT victory in 27 years when he took the Junior 600 title on a Valmoto Daytona. The following year he won the Production 1000 (now Superstock) and finished on the podium in every race he entered. This was a glorious period in Anstey's career because he won the Superstock Class ahead of Ian Lougher in 2005 and beat Ian Hutchinson in the same race the following year. He cemented his reputation as one of the finest riders of his generation by taking the Superstock Class for the fourth year in a row with a 40-second demolition of TT legend John McGuinness in 2007.

Anstey is equally prolific at the sport's other main events: between 2002 and 2007 he recorded nine wins at the prestigious North West 200. In 2002 he took the Production Race, and in 2004 he won the 600cc Supersport title (he was also leading the Superbikes until he crashed out on the final lap). He returned the following year to win the Superbikes, and took another two wins in 2006. Had he not crashed again in the Superbikes in 2007, he would have won four races instead of an impressive hat-trick. Anstey has also won the Ulster Grand Prix five times.

He returned to the Isle of Man in 2008 and won the Supersport Junior TT, although he was later disqualified because his Relentless Suzuki's exhaust cam did not conform to the regulations. Anstey put this setback behind him and demolished the opposition in the second Supersport Junior TT, breaking the lap record and finishing with an average speed of 123.04 mph. Suzuki cashed in by releasing a replica of his victorious

ANSTEY

Left: *Anstey on his way to victory in the 2007 Superstock TT on a TAS Suzuki GSX-R 1000*

GSXR–600 K8.

When Anstey lapped the Ulster Grand Prix circuit at 133.98 mph in 2010 he became the fastest rider on the world's fastest track.

Name: Bruce Anstey
Born: August 21st 1969, Wellington, New Zealand
TT Career: 1999 –
TT Wins: 9

Archibald

Adrian Archibald is from the same town as the legendary Joey Dunlop. He enjoyed immediate success on the Isle of Man when he won two races (the Duke Formula One TT on a TAS 1000 Suzuki at 123.15 mph and the Senior TT itself at 124.53 mph) on debut in 2003, a year in which he also came third in the Junior 600 TT, fourth in the Production 600 and eighth in the Production 1000cc class. The entire event was overshadowed by the death of his team-mate and lap record-holder David Jeffries during practice, however.

The following year Archibald mounted a stern challenge in the Duke Formula One race but John McGuinness was unstoppable and won by 18.6 seconds from the Northern Irishman. Archibald was a minute off the pace and could only manage fifth in the Production 1000 on his Suzuki GSX-R, and he was also a minute behind Ryan Farquhar in the Production 600. But Archibald wasn't going to let two disappointing results distract him from the main prize. He lapped the Snaefell Mountain Course at 123.81 mph and took the Blue Riband event, the Senior TT, from Bruce Anstey and Gary Carswell by half a minute and a minute respectively even though they were all on identical machines.

Archibald was again second to McGuinness in the 2005 Duke Superbike TT, but he could only manage eighth on his Suzuki 600 in the Junior A TT. The following year was even more disappointing as, having signed for Yamaha, he could only finish 11th in the Superstock TT (three minutes off the pace), 12th in the Supersport TT and 13th in the Senior TT.

He was back on his Suzuki in 2007 but was three minutes behind McGuinness and could only finish seventh in the Superbike TT, although he did improve to fifth behind McGuinness, Guy Martin, Ian Hutchinson and Ian Lougher in the Senior TT. In 2008 he came third in the Superbikes, sixth in the Superstock and ninth in the Supersport TTs. He was equally consistent in 2009, 2010 and 2011 with a hatful of top-ten finishes on his Suzuki 1000, and, although 2012 was disappointing, he may decide not to retire and could return to the Isle of Man in 2013.

Name: Adrian James Archibald
Born: October 31st, 1969, Ballymoney, Northern Ireland
TT Career: 2003 –
TT Wins: 3

Bell

His father discouraged him from racing and forced him to sell his first Sunbeam motorcycle but Artie Bell disobeyed him and bought a second-hand Norton. He was supremely gifted and rode to second place in the 1938 North West 200. As with so many riders, the war robbed him of perhaps his best years but he returned to road racing in 1946 on his pre-war Norton and clocked the fastest lap at the Cookstown 100 before winning the 1947 Ulster Grand Prix at 91.25 mph. He then won the prestigious North West 200 for the first time and travelled to the Isle of Man with high hopes. He duly delivered, finishing second to Harold Daniell in the 500cc Senior TT at 82.66 mph.

On the back of this impressive showing, Norton signed him as a works rider for the 1948 season. He delivered again, placing third behind Freddie Frith and Bob Foster in the Junior 350cc TT, and then winning the Senior TT by an incredible 11 minutes from Bill Doran and Jock Weddell, both of whom were also on Nortons. He enjoyed another strong TT campaign the following year when he came third in the Junior and fourth in the Senior TTs.

Bell took his last win on the island in 1950 in the Junior TT. It was a measure of the man that he beat rising star Geoff Duke into second place by more than a minute. Duke had his revenge in the Senior TT, however, lapping at an average of 92.37 mph and consigning Bell to second place by nearly three minutes.

Bell would surely have won many more TTs had it not been for a heavy accident at La Source hairpin in the 1950 Belgian Grand Prix at Spa-Francorchamps. Leader Carlo Bandirola braked early and was struck by the AJS Porcupine of Les Graham. Graham was thrown clear in the impact but Bell then hit the AJS and collided with a timing post, effectively ending his short but brilliant Grand Prix and road-racing career.

Name: Arthur James 'Artie' Bell
Born: September 6th 1914, Belfast, Northern Ireland
Died: August 7th 1972, Belfast
TT Career: 1947 - 1950
TT Wins: 2

Bennett

Far Right: *Alec Bennett on the course during the 1927 Senior Tourist Trophy*

Alec Bennett's parents emigrated to Canada and he didn't return to Europe until he was drafted into the Canadian Expeditionary Force during the First World War. He served as a fighter pilot and dispatch rider who was so proficient on the bike that he came to the attention of Sunbeam and Norton when hostilities ceased.

He rode his first TT in 1921 but could only manage fourth place on a Sunbeam five minutes behind Howard Davies' AJS and the Indians of Freddie Dixon and Hubert Le Vack. He collected his first win the following year in the 500cc Senior TT, however, when he rode for seven minutes shy of four hours and averaged a shade under 60 mph. He didn't make an impact in 1923 but returned in 1924 to take the 500cc Senior TT at 61.64 mph, the first time it had been won at more than a mile a minute. He came third the following year for Norton but was several minutes off the pace set by Davies on an HRD and Frank Longman on an AJS.

Bennett won the 1926 Junior TT for Velocette against the likes of Jimmie Simpson and Wal Handley at 66 mph but he couldn't place in the Senior TT until he won it again in 1927. He continued his remarkable record on the island with a win in the 1928 Junior TT at 68.65 mph, a third place the following year at 69 mph, and the runner-up spot in the Senior TT for Sunbeam at more than 70 mph.

Bennett didn't compete in 1930 or 1931 but he was back on the mountain in 1932. He was past his best, however, and could only manage eighth place in the Junior 350cc TT. Having also enjoyed enormous success on the continent (he won Grand Prix in France and Belgium, and helped team GB to a gold medal at the international six-day trial), he then decided to retire and concentrate on his motorsport business in Southampton.

> **Name:** Alec Bennett
> **Born:** April 21st 1897, County Down, Northern Ireland
> **Died:** 1973, Canada
> **TT Career:** 1921 - 1932
> **TT Wins:** 5

Boddice

Like many great TT riders before and since, Mick Boddice came from a family with a rich racing heritage. His father, Bill, was a champion sidecar racer who eventually became a steward at the festival. Mick first competed in the sidecar races in 1966 but his fuel tank was punctured by a stray bolt and he was forced to retire. The following year he came eighth but it wasn't until 1983 that he registered his first win.

In 1989, he and passenger Chas Birks smashed Jock Taylor's 1981 sidecar record, lapping at 108.31 mph from a standing start, and comfortably beat Dennis Brown and Bill Nelson. The first race saw their fuel tank split so this was a welcome return to form. In all, Boddice would win nine races and garner another 11 podiums in a glittering career. He retired from the TT in 1993.

Name: Mick Boddice
Born: 1947, Kidderminster, England
TT Career: 1966 – 1993
TT Wins: 9

Collier

Far Right:
*Charlie Collier
with his winning
motorcycle from
1907*

Charlie Collier and his brother, Henry, were the unofficial founders of road racing in the late 19th century. Their father manufactured Matchless motorcycles and Charlie began racing them unofficially in 1899. Three years later he entered a 3.5-mile race at Canning Town but he was denied victory on the last lap when his tyre burst. In 1905 the Collier brothers both entered the eliminator for the International Motorcycle Cup on the Isle of Man. Held over the Gordon Bennett course, the time trial was won by J.S. Campbell. Henry also qualified but his Matchless then suffered a broken connecting rod and he was forced to retire.

Having raced in the 1906 International Cup, Charlie entered the single-cylinder class at the 1907 Isle of Man TT. He won the race on his 431cc Matchless from the Triumphs of Jack Marshall and Frank Hulbert in 4 hours 8 minutes and 8 seconds at an average speed of 38.21 mph. The following year Marshall suffered a number of mechanical failures but Collier couldn't capitalise and eventually finished two minutes behind his rival. He watched his brother win in 1909 but then devoted much of his time to track racing and record breaking before returning to the Isle of Man for the 1910 TT.

Although H.H. Bowen took an early lead, he crashed into a wall and left the Collier brothers to battle it out for victory. Charlie eventually prevailed on his Matchless 500 at an average speed of 50.63 mph. He would have won again in 1911 had he not run out of fuel and topped up away from the pits, for which he was later disqualified. His career then gradually declined and he could only manage fourth in the 1912 Senior TT and a retirement on the first lap of the 1914 TT.

He later became managing director of both AJS and Matchless motorcycles and died at the age of 69 in 1954.

Name: Charlie Collier
Born: 1885, Plumstead, England
Died: 1954
TT Career: 1907 – 1914
TT Wins: 2

Crosby

Far Right:
*Graeme Crosby
on a Suzuki XR69*

Graeme Crosby began racing in his native New Zealand in 1974. Two years later he'd graduated to Australian Superbikes. He showed enough promise for Mike Hailwood to recommend him to the organisers of the 1979 TT, so he bypassed the usual qualification route via the Manx Grand Prix. He arrived with a highly tuned Z1 1000cc engine crammed into a Moriwaki 'Monster' chassis, but he struggled to learn the circuit and came away with a disappointing fourth place in the Formula One TT, although he did beat Hailwood.

By 1980 he'd worked his way into the 500cc road-racing World Championship on a Suzuki XR34 RGB500. He won the Senior TT on the Isle of Man on the same machine after battling it out with Ian Richards until the latter's bike failed, and he then delivered the TT Formula One World Championship (a title he defended on the Suzuki in 1981). He might have won the Formula One race had Mick Grant not managed three full laps on one tank of fuel. He then finished fifth in the 500cc World Championship behind superstars like Marco Lucchinelli, Randy Mamola, Kenny Roberts and Barry Sheene. He returned to the Isle of Man in 1981 and took a historic double in the Formula One and the Classic TTs, although Honda protested vehemently that he'd asked to change his start time and should have a penalty. The stewards overruled the protest and Crosby took a superb win.

He joined Giacomo Agostini at Yamaha in 1982 and promptly won the Daytona 200. Despite not winning a 500cc race and suffering injuries after a practice crash, he still finished with several podiums and came second in the title race to Franco Uncini. He retired from the Grand Prix circuit at the end of the season and returned to New Zealand to race touring cars. He was inducted into the New Zealand Sports Hall of Fame in 1995 and the Motorcycling Hall of Fame in 2007.

Name: Graeme Crosby
Born: 1955, New Zealand
TT Career: 1979 – 1981
TT Wins: 3

Crowe

Nick Crowe began his motorsport career as a passenger in sidecars. He finished 10th in the 1995 TT, seventh and 10th the following year (in the A and B Races respectively) and second in 1998. Two years later he graduated to the rider's seat and installed childhood friend Darren Hope in the passenger seat. They didn't have much initial success and then the 2001 TT was cancelled because of the outbreak of foot-and-mouth disease across the UK.

In fact the pairing had to wait until 2005 to record their first TT victory in Race A. Crowe and Hope brought the Honda home just two seconds ahead of Steve Norbury and Andrew Smith's Yamaha after more than an hour of racing. It was one of the closest finishes in TT history. They then came second to Dave Molyneux and Daniel Sayle in Race B, although they were over a minute off the pace. The pair stormed to victory over Norbury and Scott Parnell in the A Race in 2006 and they then made it a historic double with victory over the same pair in the B Race.

In 2007 Crowe teamed up with Dan Sayle and the pair recorded the fastest practice run with a new outright lap record that still remains. However, they had to retire from the lead in both races after mechanical failure. Crowe recruited Mark Cox as his passenger for the 2008 festival and the pair delivered

another double in the A and B Races at 114 mph.

Crowe and Cox qualified on pole for the 2009 festival and were leading Race A when they suffered a mechanical problem and were forced to retire. In the second race they crashed heavily on lap one after colliding with a hare near Ballaugh Bridge at Ballacobb and had to be airlifted to hospital with serious injuries. The race was then abandoned by the marshals. Crowe is still recovering from his injuries and has not raced at the event since.

Name: Nick Crowe	
Born: 1977, Isle of Man	
TT Career: 1995 - 2009	
TT Wins: 5	

Daniell

Harold Daniell was a talented short-circuit racer who debuted on the Isle of Man in 1930. His first win came three years later in the Manx Grand Prix so he returned the following year on a works AJS and managed a creditable ninth in the Senior TT behind legends of the sport like Jimmie Guthrie and Jimmy Simpson. He was forced to retire from the Junior 350cc event, but returned in 1935 determined to make his mark on the TT. This time he could only manage eighth in the Junior TT and a DNF in the Senior. In 1936 he fared no better, finishing ninth in the Junior and retiring his four-cylinder AJS after a mechanical failure. It was an inauspicious start to one of the great pre-war careers.

He returned in 1937 with a tuned Norton instead of the unreliable AJS and managed fifth place in both the Senior and Junior TTs. He then took the same bike to victory over Stanley Woods at Donington and Crystal Palace, and later came second at the Dutch TT. Joe Craig at Norton recognised his ability and offered him a works ride in 1938. Daniell agreed and delivered on the Isle of Man by taking the Senior TT with the first sub-25-minute lap at over 91 mph. He probably wouldn't have won the event had he not overtaken Woods on that extraordinary final lap but he scraped home by 14 seconds. His lap record would stand for 12 years.

Daniell volunteered for military service at the outbreak of the Second World War but he was rejected due to poor eyesight (!) and served in the Home Guard instead. When racing resumed on the Isle of Man in 1947, he won the Senior TT on a Norton from Artie Bell

Left: *Daniell riding an A.J.S. motorcycle during the Junior T.T. races*

at only 82.81 mph (speeds were down due to the low quality of petrol and the banning of superchargers). Bell avenged this defeat a year later when Daniell failed to finish but Daniell was back with a bang in 1949 when he took the Senior TT by more than a minute from Jonny Lockett's Norton and Ernie Lyons's Velocette. He finished sixth overall in the 500cc World Championship and also finished fourth in the Junior TT on his 350cc Norton.

Having raced successfully across the continent in 1950 he then made his last appearance at the TT. He was third in the Junior race behind Artie Bell and emerging superstar Geoff Duke, and he finished behind the pair again, as well as Jonny Lockett and Les Graham, in the Senior TT. He retired from motorcycle racing immediately and entered several Formula Three car races, although he eventually retired to become a Norton dealer in Forest Hill, London.

Name: Harold Daniell
Born: October 29th 1909, London, England
Died: January 19th 1967, London
TT Career: 1930 - 1950
TT Wins: 3

Duke

Geoff Duke first made an impact on the world of motorcycle racing when he won the 1949 Senior Clubmans TT, and he then backed it up with a win in the Senior Manx Grand Prix. He was immediately signed by Norton to ride for the factory team in the 1950 TT and he repaid the faith by coming second in the Junior TT and winning the Senior with new lap and race records. He finished the season as World Championship runner-up in both the 350cc and 500cc classes. He then swept all before him in a glorious 1951 campaign that saw him win both events at the TT as well as seven more races and both World Championships: the sport's first superstar had arrived.

He enjoyed another magnificent year in 1952 when he won every 350cc race he entered, including the TT, and took his second World Championship in that class. He had less success on the 500 and retired in the first two races. He bounced back with second places in Holland and Belgium but a lowly seventh place in the

championship persuaded him to sign for Gilera in 1953.

He delivered immediately, winning the 500cc world title, a championship he successfully defended the following year after irresistible victories in Belgium, Holland, Germany, Switzerland and Italy. He only finished second on the Isle of Man however, although he returned in 1955 to win and claim yet another 500cc world title after more victories in France, Germany and Holland. He was initially credited with being the first man to lap the mountain course at more than 100 mph but a later correction rounded his speed down to 99.97 and Bob McIntyre is now given the honour.

He would surely have claimed a fourth consecutive title had he not been banned for six months for supporting a riders' strike over start money and appearance fees. Thereafter his career gradually wound down and he rejoined Norton after an unsuccessful 1957 season with Gilera. He managed a couple of wins in Sweden in the following year's championship but

Left: *Geoff Duke taking the Quarter Bridge at high speed during the Isle of Man Senior TT Race which he won with a record speed of 92.27 mph on his Norton*

the best he could manage in the TT was a fourth place in the 350cc in 1959.

A legend in his own lifetime, Duke was the first man to race in a one-piece leather suit, and his 33 wins from 89 Grand Prix starts, six world titles and six TT wins elevate him to the pinnacle of his profession. He was named sportsman of the year in 1951, was awarded the Seagrave Trophy for his outstanding contribution to motorsport, and was then given an OBE in 1953. Three bends at the 32-mile mark on the Snaefell Mountain Course are now known as Duke's and the FIM named him as a Grand Prix Legend in 2002. His son, Peter, founded Duke Video in 1981 to promote and distribute motorsport DVDs to a global audience.

Name: Geoffrey Ernest Duke, OBE
Born: March 29th 1923, St Helens, England
TT Career: 1949 - 1959
TT Wins: 6

Dunlop, Joey

Although Joey Dunlop competed in the World Grand Prix Championships, the World Formula 750 series and World Superbikes, he was best known for his motorcycle road racing at the Isle of Man TT and the Ulster Grand Prix. He first competed on the island in 1976 but he didn't finish either the Lightweight 250cc or the Classic and only came 16th in the Junior TT and 18th in the Senior event.

The following year he won the Jubilee TT, the first of 26 victories over the next quarter of a century. He recorded his first hat-trick (Junior, Formula One and Senior TTs) in 1985 and repeated the feat three years later. He was the dominant rider throughout the next decade, winning at least one event every year from 1992 (Ultra Lightweight) to 1998 (Lightweight). Two years later he notched his third and final hat-trick with wins in the Ultra-Lightweight, Lightweight and Formula One classes.

His life outside racing was equally eventful. While heading from Strangford to the Isle of Man in 1985 the ship struck St Patrick's Rock, lost its rudder and eventually sank after colliding with St Angus Rock. The Portaferry lifeboat rescued everyone on board and the cargo of motorbikes was also salvaged. Dunlop was also a tireless charity worker who took tonnes of aid to underprivileged children in Romania and the war-ravaged Balkan States. He said that receiving an OBE for services to charity meant more than any of his achievements in bike racing.

In 2000 Dunlop won a 600cc and then a 750cc race on the Pirita-Kose-Kloostrimetsa Circuit in Estonia. While leading the subsequent 125cc event he appeared to lose control and collided with trees on the track apron. He was killed instantly. Fifty thousand mourners attended his funeral and a memorial statue was erected in Ballymoney.

The most successful TT rider at the annual event is now awarded the Joey Dunlop Cup, and a second statue of Dunlop on his Honda overlooks 'Joey's'

Left: *Joey Dunlop riding in the 1981 Isle of Man TT*

at Bungalow Bend at the 26th mile marker on the TT course. Having also won the Formula One TT Championship five times in a row (1982–86) and the Ulster Grand Prix 24 times between 1979 and 1999, this incomparable champion remains the benchmark for all other TT riders. In 2005 Motorcycle News voted him the fifth most influential motorcycling icon in history, and four years later he was named the third greatest Irish sportsman of all time.

Name: William Joseph 'Joey' Dunlop, OBE
Born: February 25th 1952, Ballymoney, Northern Ireland
Died: July 2nd 2000, Tallinn, Estonia
TT Career: 1976 – 2000
TT Wins: 26

Dunlop, Michael

Michael Dunlop is the son of the former TT star Robert. He made his debut at the TT in 2007 but could only manage 25th in the Superbike class and didn't finish either the Supersport or Senior TTs. He fared little better in his second year, although he did finish in the top ten of the Supersport Junior Race 1 and Supersport Junior Race 2 TTs as well as the Senior TT. In the latter he managed a lap at 124.77 mph and thus became the fastest Dunlop ever on the Snaefell Mountain Course. He failed to finish the Lightweight 250cc or Superstock TTs but he did manage 14th in the Superbikes. It had been a difficult decision to travel to the Isle of Man because his father had been killed at the North West 200 earlier in the year. Michael somehow put his grief on hold, however, and won the 250cc event, so it was perhaps no surprise that he chose to compete in the TT.

By 2009, Dunlop was familiar with the course and he finished second in both Lightweight 250cc races to Ian Lougher. He didn't finish the Superstock, Superbike, Senior or Supersport Race 1 TTs but he finally registered his first win on the island in the Supersport Junior Race 2 on a Yamaha 600. He won by half a minute from Bruce Anstey's Suzuki and Conor Cummins's Kawasaki.

Dunlop was solid if not spectacular the following year: he didn't win a race but he took podiums in both Supersport races and came second to Ian Hutchinson in the Superbike TT at an average speed over the 37.73-mile course of 126.83 mph. In 2011 he recorded his second TT win when he took the Superstock title ahead of John McGuinness at 127.13 mph. He also managed a fifth in the Superbike TT on a 1000cc Kawasaki, although he was three minutes off the pace set by McGuinness on the Honda. He battled hard in the Senior TT but McGuinness was again in a class of his own and won from Guy Martin, Bruce Anstey, Cameron Donald, Keith Amor and then Dunlop.

He took his third TT win in 2012

(Dunlop also has three Manx Grand Prix wins on the same course) when he took the Supersport Junior Race 2 title on his 600cc Yamaha at 124.54 mph. He also came second to McGuinness in the Superstock TT by just eight seconds but he could only manage 10th in the Superbike TT after being four minutes off McGuinness's pace. The Senior TT was then cancelled for the first time in its 105-year history due to persistent bad weather.

Dunlop looks set to uphold the family tradition and win many more races on the island if he can keep himself fit and secure reliable machinery.

Name: Michael Dunlop
Born: April 10th 1989, Northern Ireland
TT Career: 2007 –
TT Wins: 3

Dunlop, Robert

Robert Dunlop made his debut in 1979 at the Temple 100 but he had to wait two years before being sponsored to ride as a professional at Aghadowey. His career then blossomed and he won eight times at the Cookstown 100. He also won the 1989 Macau Grand Prix against Phillip McCallen and Steve Hislop's 750cc Hondas despite only riding a 500.

He enjoyed immediate success on the Isle of Man when he took the 1983 Newcomers' 350cc Manx Grand Prix but he had to wait another six years before taking the 125cc TT with a new lap record at 103.02 mph. He won the same event the following year and made it a treble in 1991, a year in which he also doubled up to win the Junior TT. He was also on the podium for both the 1992 Junior and Senior TTs, and he finished second in the 1993 125cc event.

He suffered career-threatening injuries after a big crash at Ballaugh Bridge in the 1994 Formula One TT (his rear wheel collapsed just after taking the jump) and he was out of action on the island for the next three years. It is testament to his strength of will and peak physical conditioning that he returned to racing at all, and a minor miracle that he came third in the Ultra-Lightweight race in 1997. The following year he completed his comeback by winning the Ultra-Lightweight TT, a race in which he also made the podium in 2000 and 2002. He just missed out on a podium in 2003 but finished second behind Chris Palmer in 2004. He retired from TT racing thereafter and was the first person to be inducted into the Irish Motorcycle Hall of Fame in February 2005. He then announced another comeback.

Dunlop took a record-breaking 15th win at the North West 200 in 2006 but he was killed during practice for the same event two years later. He was thrown over the handlebars at 160 mph when the engine seized and he

suffered fatal chest injuries after being struck by Darren Burns's machine. His son, Michael, won the race and dedicated the victory to his father. Robert was then laid to rest alongside Joey in Ballymoney.

Name: Robert Dunlop
Born: November 25th 1960, Northern Ireland
Died: May 15th 2008, Northern Ireland
TT Career: 1983 – 2005
TT Wins: 5

Farquhar

Ryan Farquhar enjoyed a number of high-profile wins during his early career but he couldn't take the big prizes on the Isle of Man in his first two years at the TT despite breaking the 600cc lap record in 2003. In 2004 he won the Production 600 on a Kawasaki, however, and he backed this up with third place in the Superstock and a second outright win in the Supersport TT the following year.

In 2006 Farquhar signed for Suzuki but he collided with a backmarker at the first road race of the year in Cookstown and was injured for the remainder of the season. He returned to the Isle of Man in 2007 and finished sixth in the Superbike TT and seventh in the Junior Supersport, but it would be another year before he was back to his blistering best on the Snaefell Mountain Course. He took pole position in the Junior 600cc and Superstock races but could only manage fourth place in both races and a third in Race 2 of the Juniors, although he then secured sixth place in the Superbikes, an excellent second to Ian Lougher in the Lightweight

250cc TT, and another fourth in the Senior TT where John McGuinness once again reigned supreme. Five top-six finishes on the toughest course in the world spoke volumes about this record-breaking rider.

In 2009 Farquhar's stock rose even further as he took a double at the Manx Grand Prix and then surpassed the legendary Joey Dunlop's record of 118 Irish National road-race wins with a clean sweep at Killalane. This took his total to an incredible 60 wins for the season on the KMR Kawasaki. He was then awarded the prestigious Duke Road Race Rankings Trophy for the third time. He could only finish sixth and seventh in the two Supersport 600cc TTs, however, although when he returned the following year he finished 10th in the Superbikes, ninth in the first and second Supersport races, and second to Ian Hutchinson in both the Superstock and Senior TTs.

He crashed at Keppel Gate during practice for the 2011 TT and wasn't in any condition to do better than a brave 13th in

Left: *Ryan Farquhar at the start of the 2012 Lightweight TT*

the Senior TT. In 2012 he took his third and final TT win in the Lightweight class. He also secured another podium finish with third place in the Junior Supersport TT, but the Senior TT was cancelled due to poor weather.

This supreme road racer retired when his uncle, Trevor Ferguson, was killed at the 2012 Manx Grand Prix. His record of 127 national wins, a unique five wins in a day at Cookstown and the Duke Trophy (four times) will be tough to match.

Name: Ryan Farquhar
Born: February 2nd 1976, Dungannon, Northern Ireland
TT Career: 2002 - 2012
TT Wins: 3

Fisher

Rob Fisher began his motorsport career riding in the sidecar at motocross events. He also enjoyed a brief spell as a passenger during the 1989 British Championships but he felt that he would make a better rider so he switched to the saddle and promptly won the British Championships in 1991 and 1992. He found it difficult to attract a sponsor, however, so the team disbanded.

He was then offered a seat on a Honda CBR600, but he and passenger Vince Butler only had time for one race at Donington Park before travelling to the Isle of Man for the 1993 TT. He won the Newcomer Award after finishing sixth in Race A but the petrol pump failed in Race B and put an end to their hopes of a podium finish. He returned the following year with Mick Wynn in the sidecar, however.

The pair won two TT races using a stock FZR600 and Fisher retained his titles with Boyd Hutchinson providing ballast and balance in 1995. The week wasn't without incident, however: Race A saw them break the lap record and they were on course for an even faster time in Race B when they crashed into the wall at 80 mph coming into May Hill. Hutchinson was launched up the middle of the road while Fisher grazed the wall.

They just missed out on the top spot to archrival Dave Molyneux in 1996, and, although they were back on top of the podium in 1997, it was only in Race B because the engine had self-destructed in Race A. In 1999 Fisher came second in Race A but then won Race B, and the following year he completed his third double on his Baker Honda 600 with a new lap record at 110.71 mph. With new partner Rick Long, the pair continued to rack up the victories until 'The Fisher King's' 10th and last in Race B in 2002.

Name: Robert Fisher
Born: 1970, Workington, England
TT Career: 1993 - 2002
TT Wins: 10

Fogarty

Carl Fogarty entered and won the 1985 Lightweight Manx Newcomers' Grand Prix but he had to wait another four years before recording his first TT win in the Production 750. He'd already been crowned TT Formula One World Champion but he then had an epic dice with Honda team-mate Steve Hislop and Dave Leach's Yamaha. Fogarty gambled on an early pit-stop and held out for victory by 1.8 seconds despite a late Leach charge across the mountains.

In 1990, Fogarty was at his peak and he duly won the Formula One TT on a Silkolene Honda at 118.35 mph from Nick Jeffries's Yamaha and Robert Dunlop's JPS Norton. He came fourth in the Junior TT behind Eddie Laycock, Steve Hislop and Ian Lougher but couldn't finish the Supersport 600. He bounced back with a superb second place to Dave Leach in the Supersport 400 (losing by just eight seconds) before he took his second win of the festival in the Senior TT. It was a thoroughly dominant performance and

he won by over a minute from Trevor Nation's Honda and two minutes from Dave Leach in third.

He'd toyed with a World Superbike career in 1988 and 1989, and he then raced six times in the 1990 season, but he met with little success. In 1991 he threw himself into the championship on a Honda and 18 top-ten finishes saw him place seventh in the championship. He also managed second to Steve Hislop in the Formula One TT, although he didn't finish the following year. He did, however, finish runner-up to Hislop in the 1992 Senior TT, a year in which he set the outright lap record of 18 minutes 18.8 seconds (123.61 mph), which wasn't broken until Jim Moodie cracked it on a Honda RC45 in 1999.

Fogarty won his first Superbike race on a Ducati at Donington in 1992 but it wasn't until the following year that he recorded multiple victories. Despite winning twice as many races as Scott Russell, the latter's consistency saw him take the title. Fogarty reversed their

positions the following year and took a second world title in 1995 with 13 irresistible victories. He then signed for Honda but could only win four races in 1996 and finished fourth overall behind Troy Corser, Aaron Slight and John Kocinski. He was runner-up to Kocinski in 1997 but then took two more world titles for Ducati.

He was forced to retire in 2000 after his shoulder refused to heal following a crash at Philip Island. Two years later he founded the Foggy Petronas World Superbike team with Corser and James Haydon in the saddle but the machines weren't competitive and could only manage a couple of podiums.

Name: Carl George Fogarty, MBE
Born: July 1st 1965, Blackburn, England
TT Career: 1985 - 1992
TT Wins: 3

Frith

Freddie Frith started his working life as a stonemason but he then moved into the motor trade and entered the Junior Manx Grand Prix in 1935. He duly won the event and joined Norton for the next festival. It was a perfect combination as he took the Junior TT and came second in the Senior. He then added the European 350cc title. In 1937 he raised the record average speed on the Snaefell Mountain Course to over 90 mph, an incredible feat given the condition of the roads and the relatively primitive motorcycles of the period. He duly won the Senior TT but could only finish third in both the Junior 350cc and Senior 500cc classes the following year. He finished third again in the 1939 Senior TT and was then robbed of his best years by the outbreak of World War Two. Frith served in the Infantry Driving & Maintenance School teaching officers how to ride cross-country on 500cc Nortons.

Racing didn't resume on the Isle of Man until 1947 and Frith missed out in his first TT for eight years after coming off his 500cc Moto Guzzi. He bounced back and won

the 1948 Junior 350cc for Velocette by five minutes from Bob Foster and Artie Bell. He repeated the win in the Junior 350cc class in 1949, by which time the event had been incorporated into the inaugural Grand Prix

World Championship. Frith won every 350cc race of the season and was crowned World Champion after the Ulster Grand Prix. He also finished fifth at the Swiss Grand Prix in the 500cc class.

Name: Frederick Lee 'Freddie' Frith
Born: May 30th 1909, Grimsby, England
Died: May 24th 1988, Grimsby
TT Career: 1935 - 1949
TT Wins: 5

Above: *Frith on a Norton*

Grant

A soft-spoken and down-to-earth Yorkshireman, Mick Grant provided a sharp contrast to Barry Sheene, with the Londoner living the playboy lifestyle. He first competed at the TT in 1970 but he could only manage 18th place on a Yamaha and he had to wait another couple of years to record his first podiums – he finished third in the Junior TT on a Yamaha and third in the Senior TT on a Kawasaki. He also teamed up with Dave Croxford to take the Thruxton 500 endurance title.

He finally won on the Isle of Man in the 750cc Production event in 1974 on a Triumph, and he then smashed Mike Hailwood's eight-year-old lap record the following year during the Classic. He monstered the track at an average speed of 109.82 mph, and, although he eventually retired, the lap record and a Senior TT win on a 500cc Kawasaki meant the week wasn't a dead loss.

In 1977 he could only manage seventh place in the Junior 250cc TT but he then won the Classic TT by a full four minutes at 110.76 mph on a Kawasaki. The following year he demolished the opposition by two minutes in the Classic, but 1979 was a poor festival and he didn't manage a podium.

He returned in 1980 with a bang and won the Formula One TT on a Honda by only ten seconds from Graeme Crosby's Suzuki and Sam McClements's Honda. He lost out to the legendary Joey Dunlop in the Classic TT by a matter of seconds, and he missed out in the same event to Crosby (with both men on Suzukis) the following year, although he did then take the main event, the 1981 Senior TT ahead of Donny Robinson and John Newbold.

He didn't make any impact in 1982 but returned in 1983 to take second place in the Formula One TT behind Dunlop, although he could only manage fifth in the Senior TT. He took yet another podium for a third-place finish in the 1984 Classic TT (behind Rob McElnea and Dunlop) but could only manage sixth in the Production 750cc+ class and the Senior TT. Later that year

Left: *Mick Grant at the 1975 North West 200*

he won the Macau Grand Prix for the second time.

Grant's last win on the island came in the 1985 Production 750cc event for Heron Suzuki at 104.36 mph but he missed out completely in the Senior TT. In all, he won seven TTs and remains one of the most influential riders of the 1970s and early 1980s. He retired from Grand Prix motorcycling in 1984 and contested his last TT the following year.

Name: Mick Grant
Born: July 10th 1944, Yorkshire, England
TT Career: 1970 – 1985
TT Wins: 7

Guthrie

Jimmy Guthrie made his debut on the Snaefell Mountain Course in 1923 but there was nothing about his performance that hinted at the greatness to come. He retired his Matchless motorcycle from the Junior Race at Kirk Michael with valve problems on the first lap. He didn't reappear at the TT for four years and he had to retire his Hudson from the Junior race on lap five at Ballacraine when the petrol pipe ruptured. He rode magnificently in the Senior TT, however, and was rewarded with a fine second place to Alec Bennett at an average speed of 66 mph.

He was trailing Bennett again in the 1928 Junior TT when his Norton backfired and ignited a fuel spill while he was in the pits. He was forced to retire from the race and suffered the same fate in the Senior TT when his Norton failed him at Kirk Michael on the first lap. He was badly injured in a crash as Greeba Bridge during practice for the 1929 TT and failed to make the start line for either the Senior or Junior events, although he finally won his first TT the following year in the Lightweight class on an AJS at 64.71 mph. He was again unlucky in the Senior and Junior TTs however, as mechanical failures forced him to retire from both.

Guthrie broke five world speed records on his Norton International at the Montlhéry Bowl in France between the 1930 and 1931 TTs, but he could only finish second to team-mate Percy Hunt in both classes on the island. The following year he struck and killed a sheep during practice. He then came off at Governor's Bridge in the Junior class and missed out to Stanley Woods in the Senior TT (which gave Woods his first double). Woods doubled up again in 1933 after Guthrie came off in the Junior race and the Scotsman could only finish fourth to Norton team-mates Woods, Hunt and Jimmie Simpson in the Senior TT.

Guthrie inherited the team leader's position from Woods when the latter joined Moto Guzzi after an argument over prize money. He promptly won the 1934 500cc North West 200 and

Left: *Jimmy Guthrie push-starts his Model 40 Norton at the 1933 TT*

then doubled up at the Isle of Man. He repeated his North West 200 win in 1935 and then took the Junior TT at 79.14 mph. The event was used as a backdrop for the George Formby film No Limit, and the Senior TT was packed with a drama all its own: Guthrie built up a lead of 26 seconds over Stanley Woods and, as the pit crew came out to refuel the Moto Guzzi rider, Guthrie's Norton team signalled for him to take it easy on the last lap because Woods's refuelling would put him completely out of touch. Woods had other ideas though and went straight through without refuelling. It was a big risk but it paid off as he set the outright lap record. The Norton team called their signal station in Ramsey to tell Guthrie to up the pace but Woods's magnificent lap saw him take the title by four seconds.

Woods was controversially disqualified and then reinstated at the 1936 Junior TT for receiving help replacing his broken drive train, but he left no room for doubt in the Senior TT and avenged his defeat by Woods the previous year. He won the Junior race in 1937 but was forced to retire from the Senior TT. In all, he recorded six wins and five second places on the island. He may well have gone on to win many more TTs but this supremely talented rider was killed after crashing at the 1937 German Grand Prix.

Name: Andrew James 'Jimmy' Guthrie
Born: May 23rd 1897, Hawick, Scotland
Died: August 8th 1937, Hohenstein-Ernstthal, Germany
TT Career: 1923 – 1937
TT Wins: 6

Hailwood

Mike Hailwood's father was a successful motorcycle dealer so he learned to ride at a young age in a field. He left college early and went to work for Triumph after a brief stint with his dad's business. He entered his first race at Oulton Park in 1957 at the tender age of 17 but he could only finish 11th. A year later he teamed up with Dan Shorey and the pair won the Thruxton 500 Endurance Race. In 1959 he won his first Grand Prix in Ulster on a 125cc Ducati. This brought him to the attention of Japanese manufacturer Honda and he signed for them before the 1961 TT. He then became the first man to win three races in a week when he took the 125cc, 250cc and 500cc classes. He was leading a fourth race when his 350 AJS let him down. He backed up this incredible display by winning the 1961 250cc World Championship for Honda.

Hailwood was the dominant TT rider in the 1960s but he was equally prolific in Grand Prix racing. He won four consecutive 500cc World Championships for MV Agusta before returning to Honda and securing another four world titles in the 250cc and 350cc classes. In 1967 he won what is still considered the greatest time trial of all time, the Senior TT against his old rival Giacomo Agostini, but it took a lap record of 108.77 mph to see off the Italian, a mark that would last for eight years. He was expected to add to his 12 titles on the island but Honda then unexpectedly withdrew from Grand Prix racing. Rather than lose Hailwood to a rival team, Honda paid him an enormous retainer. Hailwood knew no other team could compete against MV Agusta anyway so he turned his attention to car racing.

He couldn't achieve the same level of success on four wheels, although he raced briefly in Formula One (he came third at the 1974 South African Grand Prix) and World Sports Cars. He finished on the podium at Le Mans in 1969 alongside David Hobbs in the John Wyer Ford GT40, and then succeeded Ronnie

Left: *The legendary Mike Hailwood at the 1967 Tourist Trophy*

Peterson as the 1972 European Formula Two Champion. During the 1973 South African Grand Prix, Hailwood and Clay Regazzoni collided and the Swiss driver's car went up in flames. Hailwood pulled Regazzoni from the burning wreck even though his own racing suit had caught fire. He was awarded the George Medal for his bravery. Having been injured at the 1974 German Grand Prix at the fearsome Nürburgring, Hailwood retired from Formula One and seemed ready to embrace retirement.

Four years later at the age of 38, Hailwood surprised the racing world by announcing a comeback. Few people believed he would still be competitive on the mountain course on the Isle of Man

Above: *Mike Hailwood on his 125cc Honda at the 1961 TT*

but Hailwood was no ordinary bike rider. It is testament to his skill and bravery that he won the Formula One TT by two minutes from John Williams. The following year he iced the cake with an extraordinary Senior TT win, his 14th title on the island. He missed out on a double in the Unlimited Classic to Alex George by just two seconds.

He retired for good in 1979 and established a Honda dealership in Birmingham with business partner Rodney Gould. On Saturday 21st March 1981 he set off to buy fish and chips with his children, David and Michelle. As they returned, a truck made an illegal turn across the carriageway and Hailwood could not avoid the collision. His daughter was killed instantly. Mike died two days later from his injuries, although David somehow survived relatively unscathed.

Hailwood was so far ahead of his rivals that he surely ranks as one of the all-time greats on two wheels. On

his MV Agusta he won every race bar one of the 1963 500cc championship; he then won seven from seven in the same championship the following year and repeated the clean sweep in 1965; in 1966 he won all ten rounds of the 250cc World Championship on a Honda; and in 1967 he won every race he entered in the 350cc Championship. He retired with 76 Grand Prix victories, 14 TTs, nine World Championships and in 1979 he was awarded the prestigious Seagrave Trophy (named after the former land speed record-holder). In 1981 part of the TT course was renamed Hailwood's Height.

Name: Stanley Michael Bailey 'Mike' Hailwood, MBE, GM
Born: April 2nd 1940, Oxfordshire, England
Died: March 23rd 1981, Warwickshire
TT Career: 1958 – 1979
TT Wins: 14

Handley

Wal Handley was hired as a motorcycle messenger for OK-Supreme and he rode in the 1922 TT for the company in the Lightweight class. In heavy mist he accidentally turned the wrong way onto the course and was only prevented from careering into oncoming traffic at Governor's Bridge by an alert marshal. He set the fastest lap (51 mph) but mechanical problems forced him out of the race. He entered again the following year but could only manage eighth in the Lightweight and a DNF in the Junior TT.

He then joined Rex-Acme Motorcycles but had to wait until 1925 before recording his first victories in the Junior and Super-Lightweight TTs, the first time anyone had managed a double. Had he not been forced to retire from the Lightweight TT he might have registered the first hat-trick. He finally won the Lightweight in 1927 and took the prestigious Senior TT in 1930 on a 500cc Rudge. He continued racing at

the TT until 1934 and collected another two podiums.

In 1937 he lapped Brooklands in an alcohol-fuelled BSA Empire Star at 107.6 mph but Handley was also an accomplished car racer who drove Rileys, MGs and Alfa Romeos in a

golden age of speed. He was killed when his Air Transport Auxiliary Bell Airacobra crashed shortly after take-off from RAF Kirkbride in Cumbria in 1941. The plane struggled to gain altitude and then came down in a field and exploded.

Name: Walter Leslie 'Wal' Handley
Born: April 5th 1902, Birmingham, England
Died: November 15th 1941, RAF Kirkbride
TT Career: 1922 - 1934
TT Wins: 4

Herron

Tom Herron was a road-racing specialist who began his career on the streets of Ireland in 1965. Five years later he won his first professional race in the 350cc class at the North West 200. Later that year he finished 13th in the Lightweight 250cc TT on the Isle of Man but he crashed in the Junior TT at Ballacraine and his injuries kept him out for the rest of the season. In 1971 he returned to action at the North West 200 but another crash saw him miss the TT. More bad luck dogged him in 1972 when mechanical failures ruled him out of all three races. In fact it took him until 1974 to record his first podium in the 125cc class, a feat he matched in the Junior TT the following year.

By 1976 he was familiar with the course and was on a reliable 500cc Yamaha. In one of the closest finishes in the history of the event he broke the lap record (112.27 mph) and edged out Ian Richards's Yamaha in the Senior TT by just 3.4 seconds. He'd already won the Lightweight 250cc TT ahead of Takazumi Katayama and Chas Mortimer, and he also finished a surprise fifth in the 1000cc Classic TT.

Herron managed another two podium finishes in 1977 when he came second to Phil Read's Suzuki in the Senior TT and third behind the Yamahas of Charlie Williams and Ian Richards in the Junior TT. He won a double at the 1978 North West 200 and ran returning hero Mike Hailwood close in the Formula One TT before mechanical failure ruled him out on lap three. He put the disappointment behind him and promptly won the Senior TT in a record time on an RG500 Suzuki after another epic battle with American Pat Hennon. He then rounded off a magnificent festival by finishing third in the Junior TT.

Throughout the 1970s he'd impressed as a privateer – he finished fourth in the 1976 250cc and 350cc World Championships, second in the 1977 title race, and fifth (250cc) and sixth (350cc) in 1978 – and on the back of these performances against the works teams with their big budgets he was signed by Suzuki alongside Barry Sheene

and Steve Parrish in 1979. He began the 500cc World Championship strongly but he was killed when fighting for third place having returned home to race in the North West 200. Two other riders – Brian Hamilton and Frank Kennedy – also lost their lives on 'Black Saturday'.

Name: Tom Herron
Born: December 14th 1948, Lisburn, Northern Ireland
Died: May 26th 1979, Coleraine, Northern Ireland
TT Career: 1970 - 1979
TT Wins: 3

Hislop

Steve Hislop endured his share of personal tragedy before making it as one of the greatest TT riders of all time. His father encouraged him to take up bike racing but when his younger brother and best friend Garry was killed aged only 19, and then his father died from a heart attack in 1985, young Steve slipped into an alcoholic depression. He turned his fortunes around by entering and finishing second in the Newcomers' Race at the Manx Grand Prix. He developed into a rider of considerable talent and won the 250cc British Championship, but it is for his performances on the Isle of Man that he is most fondly remembered.

He entered the TT in 1985 in the Formula One, the Classic and the 750cc categories, but he didn't make much of an impact. The following year he came third in the British class, and in 1987 he finally won his first TT, the Formula Two on a private 350cc Yamaha. He signed for Honda for their circuit season but returned to the Isle of Man to win the Formula One, Senior and 600cc TTs, the former at more than 120 mph.

Hislop and archrival Carl Fogarty had dominated the 1991 event on their Honda RVFs but neither had been expected to return in 1992. Hislop decided to enter at the last minute on an inferior Norton 588 supplied by Ron Haslam while Fogarty rode a Loctite Yamaha. John Player were supposed to sponsor Hislop but they pulled out leaving Abus to foot the bill.

Hislop defied the odds to take an unexpected second place in the Formula One class but the team had to make several aerodynamic adjustments before the Senior TT to protect Hislop from the wind. Fogarty started fourth while Hislop, starting 19th, would have to cope with far more traffic. The race developed into an epic battle with both men smashing the lap record and staying within seven seconds of one another throughout the six-lap duel. Hislop led into the last lap but Fogarty again raised the average speed to beyond 123 mph in a last-ditch effort to beat the Scot. Hislop responded with a time that was just quick enough to secure an historic TT win.

(Fogarty's death-defying hot lap remained the quickest ever for seven years.)

In 1995 Hislop graduated to Superbikes and won the British Championship on a Ducati. The team sacked him in 1997 and he then lost his place with Yamaha. The following year Kawasaki sacked him mid-season and his run of bad luck continued when he suffered a huge crash in the World Superbikes at Brands Hatch. He was struck twice in the head by his bike as he cart-wheeled through the air and, although he signed himself out of hospital later that day he was then found to have a broken neck. He made a miraculous recovery, however, and won the 2002 British Superbike Championship.

Hislop was seen by some as a self-destructive and flawed genius whose faults prevented him from succeeding on the world stage when the talent was clearly there. We will never know if he could have achieved greater success in the twilight of his career because he was killed in a helicopter crash in the summer of 2003.

Name: Robert Steven Hislop
Born: January 11th 1962, Hawick, Scotland
Died: July 30th 2003, Roxburghshire, Scotland
TT Career: 1984 - 1994
TT Wins: 11

Hutchinson

Ian Hutchinson first raced on the island in the 2003 Manx Grand Prix. He won the Newcomers' Race on his 600cc Honda despite going up against 750cc Suzukis. He returned the following year for the TT proper on a Suzuki but he could only manage a single top-ten finish in the Formula One class. Having competed in the British Superstock Championship, he entered the 2005 TT and finished the week with three top-ten finishes.

He made a breakthrough in 2006 when he signed for McAdoo Kawasaki and immediately won the 600cc North West 200. He notched two second places and a third at that year's TT, although one of the results was stripped after the bike was found to breach technical regulations. Having served his apprenticeship, Hutchinson was now ready for a major assault on the Isle of Man. He switched to HM Plant Honda and won the Supersport Junior TT from John McGuinness by only three seconds. He also managed another three podium finishes, then took his first win at the Ulster Grand Prix on a Superbike.

By 2008 Hutchinson was a major force on the road-racing circuit, but an ill-advised move to AIM Racing meant he could only manage two podiums on the Isle of Man (Junior Supersport and Senior TT). The following year he finished fourth in the Superbike TT behind McGuinness, Steve Plater and Guy Martin, but he then won the Junior and Superstock TTs. He might have won the Senior had he not come off his bike due to oil on the circuit at Quarter Bridge.

Having won the second Supersport race at the North West 200, Hutchinson was expected to do well in 2010 but no one could predict what happened next: he won the Superbike, Supersport and Superstock TTs, becoming one of the select few riders to complete a hat-trick of wins at the same event. In the second Supersport race he edged out Michael Dunlop by a whisker to equal Phillip McCallen's 1996 record of four TT victories. He then completed a historic clean sweep by taking the Senior TT,

although the event had to be shortened after Guy Martin's huge crash and a number of other retirements. This could not detract from one of the sport's great moments, however.

If this had been his annus mirabilis, then 2011 was his annus horribilis. At the end of 2010 he fell in poor conditions during a Supersport race at Silverstone and he was then struck by another bike as he lay on the track. He suffered compound fractures to his left leg and was forced to withdraw from the North West 200 and the 2011 TT, although he did ride a few exhibition laps to thank his well-wishers. His rehabilitation was complete when he brought his Swan Yamaha home in third place at the demanding Macau Grand Prix.

He faced another setback, however, when he twisted his knee in the off-season. He managed to make the North West 200 and finished a creditable seventh in the Superbike race. He still wasn't back to full fitness at the TT but he rode to a brave eighth place in the Superbike TT, ninth in the first Supersport 600cc, sixth in the second and 11th in the Superstock. The Blue Riband event, the Senior TT, was then cancelled due to bad weather for the first time in its 105-year history.

> **Name:** Ian Hutchinson
> **Born:** August 12th 1979, West Yorkshire, England
> **TT Career:** 2004 –
> **TT Wins:** 8

Jeffries

David Jeffries was born in Yorkshire into a family steeped in the tradition of motorcycle racing, particularly at the TT. His father, Tony, had won on the island in 1971 and his uncle, Nick, was also a TT winner. David was a talented youngster who competed in the 1993 World Championship, as well as World Superbikes in 1993 and 1995. He was also the British Superstock 1000 Champion twice and was a street-racing specialist who won four times at the prestigious North West 200.

Jeffries was an aggressive rider who made an immediate impact on the TT, and he was the first man to win hat-tricks at three consecutive festivals. He won his first race, the 1999 Formula One TT, and then backed it up in 2000 with victory in the Junior 600 on a V&M Yamaha (ahead of such names as Ian Lougher, Joey Dunlop and Michael Rutter); victory in the Production TT on a Yamaha R1 (ahead of Rutter again);

and victory in the Senior TT, also on an R1 (over the sport's biggest names: Rutter, Dunlop and McGuinness).

He became the first man to lap the 37.73-mile Snaefell Mountain Course at more than 125 mph (201 km/h) and set the absolute record for the circuit at an average speed of 127.29 mph during the 2002 Senior TT, which he won from Ian Lougher and John McGuinness, although McGuinness has now reclaimed the record. He also won the Formula One Race from McGuinness and Jim Moodie earlier in the week.

During practice for the 2003 TT, Daniel Janson's Suzuki GSX-R1000 sprayed oil on the gradual left turn at Crosby when its engine failed. A couple of minutes later, Jeffries approached the bend at 160 mph on his TAS Racing GSX-R, tipped the bike into the turn and lost control on the oil. Jeffries was killed instantly after colliding with a wall. The bike then brought down a telephone pole and its lines almost

garrotted Jim Moodie when he entered the bend shortly afterwards. Moodie was incredibly lucky to survive but he retired immediately. Jeffries was honoured with a parade of thousands of riders at the end of the festival.

Name: Allan David Jeffries	
Born: September 18th 1972, West Yorkshire, England	
Died: May 29th 2003, Crosby, Isle of Man	
TT Career: 1996 – 2003	
TT Wins: 9	

Lougher

Ian Lougher was born in Cardiff and he competed in many small club motorcycle events between 1982 in Llandow and 1989. He took his first race win in 1983 at Pembrey. He then travelled to the Isle of Man to make his debut at the Manx Grand Prix, which was then the amateur version of the TT. Robert Dunlop won the Newcomers 350cc event from Steve Hislop but Ian Lougher finished a creditable third in 1 hour 29 minutes and 59 seconds at an average speed of 100.62 mph. In 1984 he finished second to Dave Roper in the 500cc Historic TT, although he was lucky to be riding after breaking his collarbone in a crash on the Mountain Mile on a 250cc Armstrong.

Lougher had to wait six years before winning his first TT, the Junior 250, after an epic battle with Steve Hislop that saw both men set new lap records. He then had to wait another six years before claiming the 750cc Production Class TT. Thereafter, however, the wins came thick and fast: 1997, 1999, 2002 and 2009 Ultra-Lightweight 125cc TT on a Honda with a lap record of 108.65 mph; 2002 Production 600cc TT on a Suzuki at 118.85 mph; 2005 Supersport Junior A 600 on a Honda at 120.93 mph; and 2008 and 2009 Lightweight 250cc TTs, also for Honda, with a best average speed of 101.17 mph.

He backed up these nine wins with second place in the Ultra-Lightweight class in 1998, then a third place at the 1999 Senior TT and a fifth in the Formula One. He also finished third in the Lightweight 250cc TT and Junior TT in 2000 for Honda and Yamaha respectively. His best average around the 37.73-mile course was 122.93 mph.

Overall, Lougher's records stack up favourably against all but the very best: he has 10 wins on the mountain course, 14 second places, 5 thirds, 9 fourths, 8 fifths and 3 sixths. He also has nine wins in the North West 200 and 42 wins at the Southern 100. Since

the Duke Road Racing Rankings were introduced in 2002, Lougher has won three times and has never been outside the top three.

Name: Ian Lougher
Born: July 10th 1963, Cardiff, Wales
TT Career: 1984 –
TT Wins: 10

Above: *Ian Lougher hunts Cameron Donald in the 2010 Supersport TT*

McIntyre

Bob McIntyre entered his first off-road races in 1948 on an Ariel Red Hunter, but he soon graduated via scrambling to road racing. His skill on all surfaces served him well and he won three of four races on a BSA at Balado Airfield. In 1952 he took the same make of bike to the Isle of Man and finished second in the Junior Clubmans TT at 80 mph. He returned later in the year on an AJS to win the Manx Junior 350cc and finish second in the Senior 500cc.

AJS gave him a works ride in 1953 after he won the 350cc class at the prestigious North West 200, and, despite retiring at the TT, he still finished a creditable eighth in the 350cc World Championship. He could only finish 14th in the Senior TT in 1954 but he was now being noticed so when AJS withdrew from the motorcycle Grand Prix circuit he signed for Potts Norton as a privateer and immediately began winning. He led four of the seven laps in the Junior TT in 1955 and looked to be on course for a win when mechanical failures forced him

to slow and hand victory to Moto Guzzi's Bill Lomas. He also managed fifth place in the Senior TT at an average of 93.83 mph, after which Giulio Carcano offered him a works Guzzi ride, which McIntyre refused. He rued the missed opportunity when more mechanical issues ruled him out of the 1956 TT but he took over from the injured Geoff Duke on a Gilera in 1957 and recorded a remarkable Junior and Senior TT double, the latter within a whisker of the magic 100 mph average.

He was in contention for the World Championship that year but a crash at the Dutch TT in Assen saw him sidelined for a couple of months and, despite a determined assault on the title – second place in Ulster and a win in Monza – his team-mate, Libero Liberati, took the championship. At the end of the season McIntyre took a Gilera round the bumpy Monza circuit at 141 mph and broke the one-hour record, which itself stood until Mike Hailwood averaged 145 at Daytona in 1964 on an MV Agusta.

He missed out on the TT in 1958

but secured his third win on the island the following year on a Norton in the Formula One TT at 97.77 mph. He also came fifth in the Senior TT. In 1960 he finished third in the Junior TT, and he raised the Lightweight lap record to 99.58 mph the following year but then his engine seized and denied him victory. His second place to the legendary Mike Hailwood in the 1961 Senior TT marked the end of a brilliant road-racing career because his 1962 outing on the island ended in mechanical failure.

He continued Grand Prix racing at circuits across Europe but he then crashed while battling for the lead during a non-championship event at Oulton Park and he died from his injuries nine days later.

> **Name:** Robert MacGregor 'Bob' McIntyre
> **Born:** November 28th 1928, Glasgow, Scotland
> **Died:** August 15th 1962, Chester, England
> **TT Career:** 1952 - 1962
> **TT Wins:** 3

McCallen

Phil McCallen was born next to the Tandragee road circuit in Northern Ireland. He raced in the 1988 Manx Grand Prix (the amateur equivalent of the TT) and made his debut at the TT in 1989 but his best result was seventh place in the Ultra-Lightweight class and he could only finish 17th in the Blue Riband Senior TT. The following year he struggled again on his Honda and could only manage a sixth place in the Junior TT. In 1991 he made the breakthrough and finished in the top five in every class – Formula One, Junior, Supersport 600, Ultra-Lightweight and Senior – including a podium in the main event.

The next year brought him two wins and a second in the Formula One, Supersport 600 and Supersport 400 respectively, although the Senior TT eluded him until 1993. He finished second in 1994, won the Formula One TT in 1995 and broke the record for most wins at the event with four in an incredible 1996. Indeed he only just missed out on a clean sweep with a fourth place in the Lightweight class after victories in the Formula One, Junior, Production

and Senior TTs. This record stood until Ian Hutchinson managed an unbelievable five wins in a week in 2010. Five must have been a lucky number for McCallen because he took five wins from six starts at the 1992 North West 200 and managed five wins in a single day at the 1996 Ulster Grand Prix.

His good form continued into 1997 and he notched another three wins in the Formula One, Production and Senior TTs. He then switched to Yamaha for his last year on the island but could only manage seventh in the Junior TT and third in the Production. Throughout his career the works teams employed him as a research and development engineer and he brought this technological and business acumen into running a successful motorcycle dealership in Lisburn having retired from the track. He remains tied for fifth place on the all-time list at the Isle of Man TT with 11 wins.

Name: Phillip McCallen
Born: 1968, Portadown, Northern Ireland
TT Career: 1989 – 1999
TT Wins: 11

McGuinness

John McGuinness's father owned a motorcycle workshop but encouraged his son to become a bricklayer. Thankfully for the motorsport world, John ignored him, although his first outing in an endurance race at Aintree on a Yamaha TZ250 bought with pocket money saved from collecting mussels saw him beaten by two female riders and only yielded a 27th-place finish. He first visited the Isle of Man in 1982 to watch his father racing and he developed a fascination with the event.

He began racing the Yamaha in the hope that one day he could compete alongside his heroes, Steve Hislop and Joey Dunlop. In 1996 he competed in his first TT but he could only finish 15th, although he did win an award for the best newcomer. Three years later he scored his first win on the island in the Lightweight 250cc category. The following year he won the Singles but he then had to wait until 2003 before taking the Lightweight 400. By 2004, however, he was the dominant force over the race fortnight.

He won three races – Formula One, Junior TT and Lightweight 400 – and scored a double the following year, which included his first Senior TT (as well as the Superbike). In 2006 he scored a second hat-trick (Senior, Superbike and Supersport) and consistently smashed the outright lap record. By the end of the festival he'd lopped 13 seconds from the benchmark and raised the average speed by two miles per hour.

The following year he became the first man to lap the circuit at more than 130 mph. He collected another Superbike and Senior TT double, and then backed this up with yet another Senior win in 2008 that saw him equal Mike Hailwood's tally of 14 victories in all classes. He moved into outright second place overall behind the legendary Joey Dunlop in 2009 with victory in the Senior TT.

The next year he failed to win an event on the island, although he did take his fifth victory in the prestigious North West 200. He was back on form in 2011 and he took the six-lap Superbike TT by nearly a

minute. He then secured another double by winning the Blue Riband event, the Senior TT. He won the Superbike race again in 2012 and then took his first Superstock TT title on an HRC Honda Fireblade (his 19th win overall), although he missed out on the Senior TT. He also made his debut in the zero emissions class, finishing a creditable second behind sparring partner Michael Rutter.

Name: John McGuinness
Born: April 16th 1972, Morecambe, England
TT Career: 1996 –
TT Wins: 19

Molyneux

Right: *Dave Molyneux*

Having lived on the Isle of Man all his life, Dave Molyneux knows the mountain course like no other. He first competed at the event in 1985 but had to wait four years for his first win in his Bregazzi Yamaha TZ750. He took the Sidecar Race A at 104.56 mph but it was another four years before he scored his first double, taking the A and B races in a 600cc Yamaha at 103 mph. He repeated the feat in 1996 with his own DMR (Dave Molyneux Racing) sidecar at 110 mph but from 1998 until 2007 he only raced 600cc DMR Hondas.

During the 2006 TT he and partner Craig Hallam were caught out at 145 mph when the airflow under the sidecar became disrupted and flipped them like a powerboat. The machine was completely destroyed in the resulting fire and the pair were unable to compete because of their injuries. Molyneux made a remarkable comeback the following year and took the A and B race double at an average of 112 mph. They would be his last victories for Honda as he then signed for Suzuki (although he was still essentially riding the DMR machine he'd designed himself). In 2009 he took his 14th TT win in the A race at 115 mph.

He didn't race in 2011 but returned in 2012 with his sidecar now powered by a Kawasaki engine. In winning the A race at 113 mph he became the first rider to be powered to victory by all four major Japanese engine manufacturers. He also won the B race, his 16th overall, which places him behind only the great Joey Dunlop (26) and John McGuinness (19) in terms of outright victories on the island.

Name: Dave Molyneux
Born: November 21st 1963, Douglas, Isle of Man
TT Career: 1985 – 2012
TT Wins: 16

Moodie

Jim Moodie was a highly skilled rider who first competed in the Isle of Man TT in 1990. He had to wait three years for his first TT wins but he then managed an impressive Supersport 400 / 600 double. He backed this up with wins in the Singles and Junior TT, and when winning the 1998 Production TT he raised the average production lap speed beyond 120 mph. The following year he broke the absolute record (124.45 mph) during the Senior TT from a standing start

Moodie was caught up in the accident that claimed the life of David Jeffries at Crosby in 2003. Jeffries lost control on spilled oil from Daniel Janson's Suzuki GSX-R1000 at around 160 mph and crashed into one of the walls bordering the course. His bike careered into a telephone pole and brought the lines down into the road. Moodie had little time to react and was almost decapitated by the lines. He was airlifted to hospital in Douglas but miraculously made a full recovery and was released the next day.

He never raced at the TT again but his records over a 13-year period are tough to match: eight wins, a further seven podiums and ten more top-ten finishes.

Name: Jim Moodie
Born: 1965, Glasgow, Scotland
TT Career: 1990 – 2003
TT Wins: 8

Mortimer

Chas Mortimer competed mainly as a privateer (his family were reasonably wealthy and he was well educated) on his Yamaha, and indeed he was the first person to record a win for the manufacturer in the 500cc Grand Prix class when he took the chequered flag in Spain in 1972. Although he began racing in 1969, it took him until the following year to register his first win on the Isle of Man. It came in the Production Lightweight event, and he then took the Lightweight 125cc class in 1971 at an average speed of 83.91 mph, two miles per hour quicker than nearest rival Börje Jansson. He won the same event the following year by an incredible seven minutes (87.49 mph) from Billy Rae and Charlie Williams. This was also his best year overall as he finished second to Kent Andersson in the 125cc World Championship.

He didn't race on the island in 1973 but he returned to take third place in the 250cc TT on his Yamaha in 1974. In 1975 he finished third in the Production TT to Dave Croxford and Alex George but he then won the Lightweight 250cc TT and finished runner-up to Charlie Williams in the Junior TT. He also finished a creditable third in the Senior TT.

In 1976 Mortimer rode to victory in the Production and Junior 350cc TTs, and he also finished on the podium in the Lightweight 250cc. This was the last time the Isle of Man would host a round of the World Championship, however.

Left: *Chas Mortimer at Donington in 1982*

With riders becoming more concerned about the safety of the Snaefell Mountain Course, and Agostini vowing never to race there again, the British round was switched to Silverstone from 1977.

Mortimer continued racing on the island until 1984 – scoring a fourth place in the 1977 1000cc Classic TT and a win and a third in the 1978 Junior and Senior TTs respectively. With eight wins overall on the fearsome circuit, Chas Mortimer remains one of the sport's icons, and he is still the only man to have won FIM World Championship Grand Prix in the 125, 250, 350, 500 and 750cc classes.

Name: Charles 'Chas' Mortimer
Born: April 14th 1949, Surrey, England
TT Career: 1969 – 1984
TT Wins: 8

Pickrell

Right: *Ray Pickrell takes flight at the TT*

Ray Pickrell was an only child who was, somewhat unusually, encouraged by his father to take up motorcycle racing. He started out on a 225cc Ambassador but graduated to sporty Norton Dominators and a BSA Gold Star for impromptu races around the backstreets of North London. In 1960 he rode the BSA to Brands Hatch and entered a free practice session, although it ended with him crashing on Paddock Hill Bend.

He wasn't deterred and bought a 500cc Manx Norton for a race at the same venue the following year. He found the going tough and served a long apprenticeship in the lower echelons of the sport. He had a big crash in 1964 and broke his thigh, and he thought his career was over until Geoff Monty arranged a sponsorship deal. His results gradually improved and dealer Paul Dunstall then offered him a ride in 1968. Pickrell won 17 races that year, of which one was the 750cc Production TT on the Isle of Man at a new record average speed of 98.13 mph.

He signed for Triumph/BSA in 1971 and won his second Production TT on his most famous bike: 'Slippery Sam'. He also shared victory with Percy Tait in the prestigious Bol d'Or 24-hour endurance race. He then had his second major accident when he came off on oil while leading Giacomo Agostini in South Africa. Despite suffering a serious back injury, Pickrell won the Production TT on 'Slippery Sam' in 1972 and backed

it up with victory in the Formula 750 TT on a Triumph, setting lap records in both events (his 750cc average of 105.68 mph was faster than Agostini's best in the Senior TT).

He had another huge accident at the last race of the year at Mallory Park. His gearbox locked at the Devil's Elbow and when he landed Tony Jeffries's bike smashed into him, shattering his pelvis and leaving him in hospital hovering between life and death for six weeks. He eventually made a good recovery, although he never raced again and died in 2006.

Name: Ray Pickrell
Born: March 16th 1938, Middlesex, England
Died: February 20th 2006
TT Career: 1968 - 1972
TT Wins: 4

Plater

Steve Plater started off on speedway ovals but then trained as a bricklayer. He returned to motorsport in 1994 and won at Cadwell Park but was quiet for the next few years until he won the 1998 British Powerbike Championship and finished second in the more prestigious British Supersport series twice, once on count-back. He then finished third at the 1999 Bol d'Or on a Kawasaki and was offered a works ride by the team in the 2000 British Superbike Championship. He finished sixth overall but then missed most of 2001 after being injured. He still collected three podiums, however. He continued to improve in 2002 and recorded two late-season wins.

He then had a couple of quiet seasons before returning to win the both Superbike races at the 2006 North West 200. He entered his first TT in 2007 and finished 10th in the Superbike standings on his Yamaha YZF R1, although he was a full five minutes off the pace of John McGuinness. He backed this up with an eighth-place finish in the Supersport Junior TT and a highly creditable seventh in the Senior TT.

For his exceptional debut, he was awarded the Newcomer of the Year.

He returned in 2008 to win the Supersport TT after Bruce Anstey was disqualified, and he then won in the same class in the British series. By 2009 he was a serious contender at the TT and he duly delivered in the Blue Riband event by setting a new race record of 128.28 mph. To prove this was no fluke, Plater also finished second to McGuinness in the Superbike TT by a whisker, fourth in Race 1 and 2 of the Supersport TT and fourth again in the Superstock TT. He then won the North West 200.

At the same event the following year he came off at Quarry Hill and broke his arm and fractured his neck. It is still unclear whether he will continue to concentrate on endurance events or return to road racing on circuits like the North West 200 and the Isle of Man's Snaefell Mountain course.

> **Name:** Steve Plater
> **Born:** August 22nd 1972, Luton, England
> **TT Career:** 2007 –
> **TT Wins:** 3

Provini

Tarquinio Provini was the son of a garage owner so he grew up around motorcycles, which he started riding at 10 and racing at 16 in 1949. Five years later he won the Motogiro of Italy and eventually graduated to Grand Prix motorcycling towards the end of the season. He won the Spanish Grand Prix on a 125cc Mondial and finished fourth in the French Grand Prix early in 1955. He then went to the Isle of Man but couldn't finish his first TT on the same bike.

In 1956 he struggled again and could only manage a third place in Germany and a second in Italy, although that did give him fourth place overall in the 125cc World Championship. He came of age in 1957 by winning three of the five rounds in the 125cc, including the Isle of Man TT on his Mondial, and being declared World Champion at the end of the season. He also won two races in the 250cc class but couldn't finish the TT.

In 1958 he signed for MV Agusta and dominated the 250cc World Championship, winning all five races, including the season-opener at the TT. He had less success in the 125s but still managed three podiums and fourth overall in the championship. In 1959 he completed the elusive 125cc and 250cc double at the Isle of Man but he finished runner-up in the World Championship in both series to compatriot Carlo Ubbiali.

MV Agusta bowed out of Grand Prix motorcycling at the end of the season so Provini signed for Moto Morini. In the

next three years his best results were a third at the TT in the 250cc class and a second in Italy, but he gradually improved and by 1963 was back to his best. He won four races and took another three podiums to finish second in the World Championship to Jim Redman by the narrowest of margins.

He signed for Benelli in 1964 but couldn't recapture the glory days and his best result was a fourth place at the TT

1965. He broke his back on the mountain course in 1966 and was forced to retire from Grand Prix motor-racing with 20 wins and 19 podiums from 50 starts.

Name: Tarquinio Provini
Born: May 29th 1933, Roveleto di Cadeo, Italy
Died: January 6th 2005
TT Career: 1955 - 1965
TT Wins: 4

Read

Phil Read was a prodigiously talented rider who vied with Hailwood and Agostini for the honours during one of the sport's golden ages. He secured his and Yamaha's first world title in the 250cc class in 1964 after wins in France, West Germany, East Germany, Ulster and Italy, and with seven wins and two second places he defended the crown the following year. Teething problems with the new four-cylinder bike meant that Hailwood stole the title in 1966 but the pair battled it out again in 1967, with Hailwood edging Read out on count-back after the two finished level on points (Hailwood had one extra win during the season).

In 1968 Yamaha wanted Read to aim for the 125cc title and let team-mate Bill Ivy go for the 250cc crown but, having duly won his championship, Read decided to push for a second title and edged Ivy out on elapsed time. Yamaha were so disappointed that they refused to renew Read's contract despite the fact that he'd delivered two World Championships in a single season.

He sat out the next two seasons because the Japanese manufacturers had withdrawn from racing but he returned to claim yet another world title (his fifth) in 1971 on a modified privateer Yamaha with no factory support. He joined Italian giants MV Agusta in 1972 and delivered two 500cc World Championships (1973, 1974). This was the last win for four-stroke machines for 30 years, although he did run Agostini close in 1975. He retired from Grand Prix racing in 1976 as the first man to win world titles in the 125, 250 and 500cc classes, and he made his last appearance on a bike at the 1982 Isle of Man TT.

The island had been good to him over the previous 20 years (he won the 1960 Senior Manx Grand Prix) and he'd racked up eight wins on the Snaefell Mountain Course, his first on his debut in the Junior TT on a Norton in 1961 and his last in the Senior TT in 1977. He also finished third on a Gilera in the 1963 Senior TT and second on an AJS in the 1964 Junior TT, but it wasn't until Yamaha came onboard in 1965 that he saw an upturn in fortunes. He enjoyed two Lightweight and three 125cc wins, but then decided to retire from the event in 1973 having joined the growing ranks of those concerned about safety. He was also rightly worried that the organisers were not doing enough to ensure any riders who did crash could be attended to quickly.

He expected a great deal of criticism from fans and marshals when he made a comeback four years later – a policeman advised him to move his van to the back of his hotel so he didn't advertise his presence in Douglas – but he won them over by securing a superb double in the Formula One and Senior TTs. A true motorcycling legend, Read competed for a quarter of a century at the highest level and added eight World Championships to his TT victories.

Above: *Phil Read in his distinctive leathers and helmet*

Name: Phillip William Read
Born: January 1st 1939, Luton, England
TT Career: 1961 – 1982
TT Wins: 8

Redman

Jim Redman emigrated to Rhodesia as a young man but that didn't stop him entering motorsport events. He first competed on the Isle of Man on a Norton in 1958 but he could only manage seventh place in the Formula One 350cc event. His performances in the latter part of 1960, particularly a third place at the Ulster Grand Prix and a second in Italy on the 250cc bike, brought him a factory ride with Honda.

Redman delivered immediately, finishing fourth in the 125cc World Championship and third in the 250cc (with two wins). The following year he won ten races and took the 250cc and 350cc world titles. This ushered in a period of total dominance, during which he won a total of 45 races and six World Championships. In 1964 he became the first rider to claim three Grand Prix wins in a single day, an achievement only matched by the legendary Mike Hailwood in 1967. No one else has since managed this

remarkable feat.

He was also sensational at the Isle of Man TT festival, taking third place in the 1960 Lightweight event and fourth in the 125cc class. The following year he managed second place in the 250cc TT but he then embarked on an extraordinary winning streak by taking

Junior and Lightweight TT doubles in 1963, 1964 and 1965. He was injured midway through the 1966 season and was forced to retire from Grand Prix motorcycling. He was awarded the MBE for services to motorsport and now lives in South Africa, although he returns to the Isle of Man every year and is a major draw on the parade laps for past champions.

Name: James Albert 'Jim' Redman, MBE
Born: November 8th 1931, London, England
TT Career: 1958 – 1966
TT Wins: 6

Reid

Brain Reid began his racing career in 1976 at the Dundrod Circuit in Killinchy on a 250cc Yamaha, but he had to wait another three years before recording his first win at Carrowdore on a 125cc Morbidelli. He competed in the Manx Grand Prix in 1978 but the engine of his Yamaha TZ250 seized during the Newcomers' Race at Ramsey and he was thrown off. Two years later he came second in the senior race on a Suzuki RG500. He first raced at the TT proper in 1981 but had little success and devoted his energy to winning the 350cc Ulster Grand Prix and then a record three Irish Road Race Championships – 250cc, 350cc and 500cc – in the same year (1982).

His next season brought little return but he finished two of four races on the island in 1984, including a third place in the 250cc TT and fourth place in the Senior TT. His star was on the rise and in 1986 he delivered on the early promise by leading from start to finish and taking the Formula Two TT at a new record speed of 109.72 mph. He then came off in the Junior race and was out for several weeks, however.

He missed out in 1987 due largely to bad luck but in 1988 he finished on the podium in the Production and Junior TTs. Ill fortune dogged him again in 1989 but 1990 saw a return to form and he won the 600cc Supersport TT as well as finishing fifth in the 400cc class. His rollercoaster career on the island continued with three mechanical failures in 1991 but he returned in 1992 to take a historic double for Loctite Yamaha in the 400cc Supersport and 250cc Junior TTs.

Having won the Junior TT again the following year, he was then involved in a serious accident during the 1994 Temple 100 that left him with serious arm and leg injuries and ultimately brought about his retirement. In all, this popular rider won 18 national championships, two world titles and five TTs and, had he not suffered more than his fair share of breakdowns, he surely would have won many more races on the island.

Name: Brian Reid
Born: 1960, Belfast, Northern Ireland
TT Career: 1981 – 1994
TT Wins: 5

Rutter, Michael

Motorcycle racing is in the Rutter family blood. Father Tony won seven TTs and numerous road and circuit races in the 1970s, and Michael has carried on the tradition. He began riding professionally in 1989 but didn't manage a full season in British Superbikes until 1993 (he also raced in the World Superbike series). Rutter finished in the top six overall until 1998 but it was a win in the wet at Donington in 1995 that showcased his talent to a wider audience. Two years later he was on the podium at the same circuit after placing third in the World Superbikes, a race which was also run in poor conditions.

His wet-weather skill became more apparent on the road and he was a regular winner at the North West 200 and the Macau Grand Prix. He first raced on the Isle of Man in 1994 but it wasn't until the following year that he placed eighth in the Senior TT. In 1996 he took third in the Formula One TT, although he retired from eighth place in the Senior event. His stock was still on the rise, however.

The following year he finished second to Phillip McCallen in the Formula One TT at 118.23 mph and third on his V&M Honda to Ian Simpson and McCallen at 117.05 mph in the Junior TT, although he then had to retire from the Senior TT.

His next road-racing season brought multiple victories: his first win at the Macau Grand Prix, another at the North West 200, the Junior TT on the Isle of Man (from Ian Simpson by seven seconds), and a second place in the Formula One TT (to Simpson by just 2.2 seconds). He took another podium in the Production TT but was half a minute off the pace of Jim Moodie's Honda CBR900.

Between 2002 and 2005 he finished second (twice) and third (twice) in the British Superbike Championship but his road-racing results easily overshadowed these solid performances: he took three podiums at the 2000 Isle of Man TT (second in the Formula One class, second in the Senior TT and third in the Production 1000), two wins at the Macau Grand Prix and three wins at the North

West 200. Between 2002 and 2008 he won a further four Macau titles and four North West 200s. He devoted the next three years to circuit racing but returned to the roads in 2011 to win another two Macau GPs and two more Isle of Man TTs in the Zero Emissions class (in so doing, he became the first man to lap the Snaefell Mountain Course at more than 100 mph on an electric bike).

In all, 'The Blade' has won 28 BSB races, 12 North West 200s, three Isle of Man TTs with a further eight podiums, and he remains the record-holder for the most wins at the Macau Grand Prix with nine.

Above: *Michael Rutter at Snetterton in 2009*

Name: Michael Karl Rutter
Born: April 18th 1972, Wordsley, England
TT Career: 1994 –
TT Wins: 3

Rutter, Tony

Tony Rutter raced at a time when the TT was in danger of losing its status as a Grand Prix event. He also competed alongside some of the greatest names in the sport: Hailwood, Agostini, Grant and Dunlop. Rutter won four Formula Two World Championships and was British 350cc champion in 1971. Two years later he won the 250cc British title on a Yamaha. He also went to the Isle of Man for the first time and immediately recorded a win in the 350cc TT. His second motorcycle Grand Prix win came at the same circuit in the same event the following year, but he could only manage fifth in the Lightweight 250cc. He did come third in the Senior TT for Yamaha, however, and he collected another third place in the Classic 750cc TT.

In 1975 Rutter came fourth in the Lightweight 250cc class and eighth in the Senior TT but 1976 was a bumper year and he came second in the 350cc event with the fastest lap, fourth in the 250cc Lightweights, third in the Classic 1000cc TT and second in the Production TT on a Suzuki. By 1977 the TT had lost its status on the Grand Prix circuit because of fears over safety and Rutter made little impact over the next two years.

He was back to his best in 1979, however, finishing second in the Senior TT for Suzuki and fourth in the Formula Three TT for Honda. In 1980 he finished well down the field in every race except the Senior TT, where he managed a creditable fifth on an underpowered Yamaha. He was back on form in 1981 and took the Formula Two TT on a Ducati by over a minute, but he was well off the pace in the Senior TT and barely scraped into the top 40. He returned with Ducati in 1982 and won the Formula Two TT again. He also took third in the Classic for Yamaha, although he was several minutes behind Denis Ireland. He then blitzed a quality field to win the 350cc TT, also for Yamaha. He secured a famous hat-trick for Ducati by winning the 1983 Formula Two TT, and he enjoyed a strong 1984 by finishing third

in the Formula One TT for the Italian marque and second in the Formula Two TT, although he only managed 10th in the Senior TT for Yamaha.

In 1985 Rutter came second in the Formula One TT for Suzuki, although he was a full five minutes off the pace of Joey Dunlop, but he then bounced back with yet another win for Ducati in the Formula Two event. He also took third place for Suzuki in the Production 750cc, although he didn't finish the Senior TT.

Rutter's career was effectively ended after a horrific crash in Barcelona later that season, although he did recover and continued to ride in the TT until 1991. By then he was past his best, however, and couldn't add to his seven TT victories or nine North West 200 titles. His son, Michael, is also an accomplished rider who has won three times on the island, most recently in the zero-emissions class in 2012.

Name: Tony Rutter
Born: September 24th 1941, Birmingham, England
TT Career: 1973 - 1991
TT Wins: 7

Saville

Below: *Dave Saville*

As a member of the Bawtry-based Brindley sidecar clan, Dave Saville first raced on the mountain course in 1968. As a last-minute replacement in the 750cc class, he finished a creditable 10th. It took him until 1985 to register his first win but he then took one or both sidecar titles for Sabre F2 Racing every year until 1990. Then, in 1993, with nine Formula Two Sidecar TT wins under his belt, a record he shares with Mick Boddice and Siegfried Schauzu (all three have now retired), tragedy struck: he had a horrendous accident at the Manx Grand Prix and was left quadriplegic.

Saville battled through intensive rehabilitation programmes for seven years in Southport's Spinal Injuries Unit before he finally returned home in 2000. Despite needing round-the-clock care, he managed to attend a fund-raising event at Sulby Glen Hotel in September 2005. The world of motorsport mourned a brave and brilliant racer when he died in early 2006.

Name: Dave Saville
Born: 1950, Bawtry, England
Died: March 7th 2006, Southport, England
TT Career: 1968 – 1993
TT Wins: 9

Schauzu

When Siegfried Schauzu retired from racing sidecars at the TT in 1976 he'd racked up a record nine victories (shared only with Mick Boddice and Dave Saville). His first, at an average speed of 91 mph, came in the 1967 TT on an immaculate BMW. He and passenger Hans Schneider wowed the crowds with their aggressive riding style that earned Schauzu the nickname 'Sideways Sid'. The same pairing won the 1968 500cc Sidecar TT by an astonishing 80 seconds that translated into an average speed nearly two miles an hour faster than the German pairing of Attenburger and Schillinger.

Schauzu and Schneider could only manage a surprise second place in the 500cc class the following year, but they made up for it with a win in the 750cc category, demolishing the English opposition by nearly four minutes. They won the same event by the same enormous margin in 1970 but were off the pace in the 500cc class and narrowly missed out on a historic double. Schauzu did win the 500cc title in 1971 and 1972, but he was runner-up in

both classes the following year. He won the 750cc class again in 1974 and then took his final win in the 1000cc in 1975. He came second in 1976 and also won the German Championship five times, but he never managed to win the Sidecar World Championship.

Above: Siegfried Schauzu and Wolfgang Kalauch on their BMW at the 1975 TT

Name: Siegfried Schauzu
Born: 1944, Duisburg, Germany
TT Career: 1967 – 1976
TT Wins: 9

Simpson

Having started racing at 16, Ian Simpson entered the British Championship two years later but he had to wait until 1994 before he won the TT Superbike class on a Duckhams Norton. The manufacturer then pulled out of racing but he still managed to win the Supersport 600cc title in 1991 and 1994, and the 1993 400cc championship. Four years later he became Production Powerbike champion.

He first entered the Isle of Man TT in 1989 but he was four minutes off the pace of Steve Hislop and could only manage 15th place in the Supersport 600 TT and a DNF in the Production 1300. He didn't race again on the island until 1993 but he was again outclassed and finished a lowly 26th in the Formula One TT. He made amends with a creditable fourth in the Supersport 600 as he was only 40 seconds behind winner Jim Moodie's Honda, and fifth in the Senior TT at 114.86 mph.

Simpson finished fourth again in the 1994 Junior TT, although he was a minute behind Joey Dunlop. He recorded his first podium in the Supersport 600 when he was runner-up on his CBR Honda to Iain Duffus's FZR Yamaha by only nine seconds but he then sat out most of the 1995 road-racing season (although he did win the Superbike class at the North West 200). He returned in 1996 to take third in the Junior TT behind Iain Duffus and winner Phil McCallen, a race he would eventually win from McCallen by half a minute the following year. He also finished seventh in the 1997 Lightweight TT, second in the Production TT, third in the Senior TT and he then crowned a fantastic week by finishing fourth in the Formula One TT at 118 mph.

If 1997 had been a good year on the island, 1998 was even better: Simpson won the Formula One TT from Michael Rutter by just two seconds, then finished seven seconds behind him in the Junior TT, managed a seventh place in the Production TT and then completed a historic double by winning the Blue Riband Senior TT by just three seconds from Bob Jackson's Kawasaki 750. He

didn't finish the Lightweight TT but that hardly mattered after a superb festival. He then won the North West 200 Superbike event to cap a glorious year.

Simpson was injury-prone, however, and after breaking both his legs four times he was forced to retire in 2001, although he occasionally appears at classic events and in parades on the Isle of Man. He then made a one-off appearance in the International Classic at the 2008 North West 200.

Name: Ian Simpson
Born: 1970, Edinburgh
TT Career: 1989 - 1998
TT Wins: 3

Surtees

John Surtees is the son of a motorbike dealer who entered his first race with his father. They won but were disqualified when John was found to be underage. He started work for Vincent in the early 1950s and was soon racing in grass-track events. In 1951, at the tender age of 17, he ran living legend Geoff Duke close at Thruxton but he had to wait another four years before being offered a contract by Norton's Joe Craig.

He repaid the faith by beating Duke at Silverstone and Brands Hatch but by then Norton were struggling financially so he signed for MV Agusta instead. He won three consecutive races in the 500cc class in 1956, including the Isle of Man TT, and was declared World Champion. His season was doubtless helped by the FIM's decision to ban Geoff Duke for six months – he'd openly protested about low prize money – but Surtees still had to deliver MV Agusta's first senior title against strong opposition.

He couldn't find the same form in 1957 and only managed second at the TT,

although he did win in Holland and came third overall. In 1958 and 1959 Surtees was untouchable, however. He won the 350cc and 500cc World Championships in both years and recorded a scarcely believable 25 consecutive victories, including four at the Isle of Man (two in each class). He could only manage second at the 1960 TT in the 350cc class but another win in Ulster brought him that year's world title. He also won the 500cc TT, which, when added to his four other victories, gave him a second World Championship in 1960, his seventh overall.

He then surprised the establishment by switching to four wheels, and he made his debut for Lotus in the Formula One Monaco Grand Prix. In only his second race (at Silverstone) he drove to an incredible second place behind defending champion Jack Brabham, and he then popped the car on pole position for his third race in Portugal. He then had two quiet seasons before signing for Ferrari in 1963. The following year he delivered

the World Championship, becoming the first – and so far only – man to win world titles on two and four wheels. He retired from motor-racing in 1972 and set up his own F1 team. Former rider Mike Hailwood promptly delivered the European Formula Two title, although the team eventually folded in 1978 after little success in the top echelons.

Surtees was the first man to win the Senior TT three times in succession, and his record of 38 Grand Prix motorcycle wins and another seven podiums from only 49 starts is unlikely to be bettered.

Name: John Surtees, OBE
Born: February 11th 1934, Tatsfield, England
TT Career: 1952 – 1960
TT Wins: 6

Taveri

Luigi Taveri debuted in the 500cc World Championship in 1954 on a Norton and he came fourth in his first race, the French Grand Prix. Later in the season he came fourth again in the 250cc class in Switzerland. He signed for Italian marque MV Agusta in 1955 and won his first 125cc race in Spain. He backed this up with three consecutive second places, including at the Isle of Man TT, before recording his second win in the 250cc event in Holland.

Having finished second to Carlo Ubbiali in the 125cc World Championship at his first attempt, he then did the same in the 250cc class the following year, 1956. In 1957 he took third on the Isle of Man behind the Italian pairing of Tarquinio Provini and Carlo Ubbiali on the 125 Agusta and second on the 250 to Cecil Sandford at 74.24 mph. He was also runner-up to Provini in the 125cc World Championship.

He sat out the TT in 1958 but returned the following year to take second place behind Provini in the Ultra-Lightweight 125cc class. He must have thought he was destined never to win on the island because he could only manage third in the 125 and eighth in the 250 TT in 1960, second in the 125 in 1961 and second behind German Ernst Degner in the Ultra-Lightweight 50cc in 1962.

His fortunes were about to change, however. Later that week he finally won his first TT, the Lightweight 125cc from Tommy Robb and Tom Phillis at a new record average speed of 89.88 mph. He took another five wins and two podiums in the remainder of the season and was finally crowned 125cc World Champion for Honda.

He was two minutes off the pace and could only manage fourth in the 1963 125cc TT, however, although a solid season saw him finish second overall in the 125cc World Championship to Hugh Anderson, fifth overall in the 250cc standings, and third behind Jim Redman and Mike Hailwood in the 350cc title race.

He was back to his best in 1964, winning five 125cc races, including the TT, and securing the World Championship with another four second places. He won again on the Isle of Man on a 50cc Honda in 1965, although he could only manage second place in the 125cc class. He ended his road-racing career with a second-place finish in the 1966 50cc TT to Ralph Bryans and the 125cc world title with five wins and three more podiums.

His three 125cc World Championships, three TT wins and seven second places, and 119 podium finishes from just 143 Grand Prix starts ensure the likeable Swiss rider will forever remain among motorcycling's elite.

Name: Luigi Taveri
Born: September 19th 1929, Horgen, Switzerland
TT Career: 1955 – 1966
TT Wins: 3

Ubbiali

Carlo Ubbiali made his debut in the sport's first professional Grand Prix year, 1949. He finished the 125cc season in fourth place for MV Agusta but then switched to Mondial for 1950. He won the first of nine world titles for the team in 1951 but, having lost out to Cecil Sandford in 1952, he re-signed for MV Agusta. He promptly won another five world 125cc titles and three 250cc crowns, which included historic doubles in 1956, 1959 and 1960. In all, he won 39 Grand Prix from just 71 starts and only failed to finish on the podium three times in his entire career.

He was equally impressive at the Isle of Man, finishing second to Cromie McCandless at his first attempt in the 125cc TT in 1951. He returned the following year on the Mondial but could only manage another second place to Cecil Sandford. He didn't make the finish of the 1953 festival but secured his third second place in 1954, this time for MV Agusta, although he trailed Ruppert Hollaus's NSU home.

In 1955 he won the Lightweight 250cc TT and he doubled up the following year with both the 125cc and 250cc titles over strong opposition from NSU and Montesa. He could only manage second place on the 125 in 1957 but the 250cc was a disappointment and he failed to finish. He was back to is best in 1958 with a win on the 125 and a second place on the 250cc Agusta. The next festival was the last to run over the shorter Clypse Course and Ubbiali could only manage a lowly fifth in the 125cc TT and second in the 250. In 1960 the event was held on the Snaefell Mountain Course and Ubbiali proved his durability and consummate skill with a win in the 125cc class and second in the 250cc TT. His record on the island is almost without equal – five wins, seven second places, one fifth and two retirements – meaning he won a third of the races he entered.

This record is perhaps even more remarkable given that he always rode within himself and never suffered a serious crash in his 12-year career. He recognised

the dangers of the sport, however, and retired at 30 while still in his prime. His nine World Championships see him ranked alongside Mike Hailwood and Valentino Rossi, and, had he continued racing, he would undoubtedly have challenged Giacomo Agostini and Ángel Nieto as the most successful riders in the history of the sport. In 2001 he was inducted into the MotoGP Hall of Fame.

Name: Carlo Ubbiali
Born: September 22nd 1929, Bergamo, Italy
TT Career: 1951 – 1960
TT Wins: 5

Williams

Charlie Williams was a superbly skilled rider who came 10th in the 500cc World Championship on a Yamaha in 1974, but he is best remembered for his performances at the Isle of Man TT. He first competed on the island in the Manx Grand Prix 1972 (which he won) and only had to wait a year before sealing his first senior victory in the Production Lightweight 250cc TT, the first of eight wins in total. He won the same event the following year and backed it up with second place in the 500cc class and a win in the 350cc class in 1975.

He missed out the following year and in 1977 the TT was dropped from the World Championship because of concerns over safety. The event went ahead anyway and he won the Junior 250cc TT and came second to Mick Grant in the 1000cc class. He won his final two TTs in 1980 after riding his Yamaha to victories in the Formula Two and Junior events.

The safety issues were raised again in 1978 after the deaths of sidecar racers Mac Hobson and Kenny Birch when their Yamaha crashed at the top of Bray Hill. Only a matter of minutes later, Swiss rider Ernst Trachsel was also killed when he came off at the bottom of the hill. It was the TT's darkest hour and the island mourned the loss deeply. The racing may have been overshadowed but there were still some brilliant moments, such as Charlie Williams's breathtaking battle with Chas Mortimer and Tom Herron in the Junior 250cc class. Williams eventually finished second.

In 1979 Williams beat Mike Hailwood and Ron Haslam but could only come second in the Formula One TT to Alex George. He then won the Junior 250cc TT on his Maxton Yamaha and came third for the same manufacturer in the Classic TT. The following year he won the Junior TT and the Formula Two TT World Championship but he then largely retired from bike racing. He has remained in the public eye by presenting the Radio

Left: *Charlie Williams*

TT Breakfast Show and joining the broadcasting teams trackside. He was also President of the TT Riders' Association in 1998.

Name: Charlie Williams
Born: July 31st 1950, Kelsall, England
TT Career: 1972 – 1980
TT Wins: 8

Woods

Stanley Woods was encouraged by pre-war Rudge works rider Tommy Green to watch the TT in 1921. Having seen the event at Hillberry he reportedly told his friends: "I can do that." And he made it his goal to return for the 1922 race. He couldn't afford a motorcycle so he wrote to the manufacturers and told them he had been offered a ride in the Junior TT if he could agree a loan deal and pay his expenses. Only the Cotton company were convinced and the 17-year-old Woods made the start having stopped to recover a set of spark plugs that had fallen out of his pocket.

His race was about to become even more eventful: he clipped the kerb at Governor's Bridge, then fell off at Sulby on lap two. He lost part of his exhaust on his next visit to the bridge and then had to cope with a pit fire. He also had to replace an exhaust valve and deal with total brake failure and another unintentional dismount at Ramsey Hairpin. Despite all the problems, he

brought the Cotton home in fifth place.

The following year Woods won the Junior TT at 55.73 mph but he then defected to rivals Norton, with whom he stayed from 1926 until 1934. In 1926 he won the Senior 500cc TT at 67.54 mph, and the following year he took four Grand Prix victories. He had to wait until 1932 before collecting both the Junior and Senior TTs, a feat he repeated in 1933. By then he was becoming disillusioned with Norton, however, so he signed for Italian manufacturer Moto Guzzi. He promptly won the Lightweight 250cc and Senior TTs, the latter at 84.68 mph. This was only the second time in the event's history that it had been won by a non-English marque (the first had been Oliver Godfrey's Indian in 1911).

His career was interrupted by the war, although by then he'd recorded his ninth and 10th TT victories: the 1938 and 1939 Junior 350cc TTs for Velocette. His career record stood until he was overtaken by Mike Hailwood

in 1965. His standing at the TT was so impressive that Woods was named the greatest of all TT riders in 1968. He died in 1993 and the Irish Post Office issued a stamp bearing his likeness three years later to commemorate the 'Irish Dasher' a true motorcycling champion who enjoyed death-defying duels with the likes of Jimmy Guthrie and Wal Handley.

Name: Stanley Woods
Born: 1903, Dublin, Ireland
Died: July 28th 1993, Dublin, Ireland
TT Career: 1921 - 1939
TT Wins: 10

Right: *Bringing your own bike is optional but encouraged*

ALSO AVAILABLE IN THE PLAYER BY PLAYER SERIES

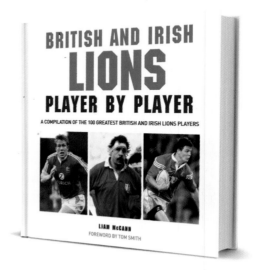

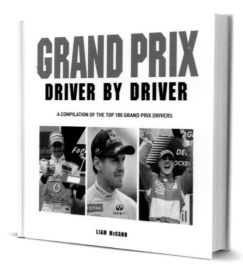

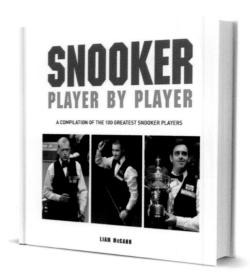

ALSO AVAILABLE IN THE PLAYER BY PLAYER SERIES

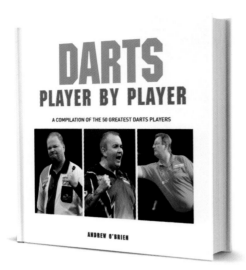

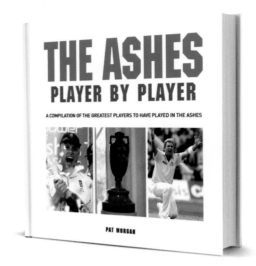

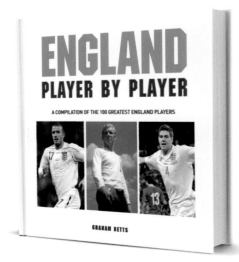

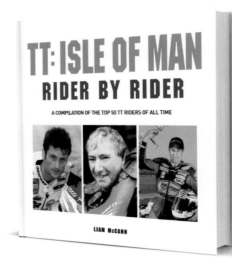

The pictures in this book were provided courtesy of the following:

GETTY IMAGES
101 Bayham Street, London NW1 0AG

WIKICOMMONS
commons.wikimedia.org

Design & Artwork by: Scott Giarnese & Alex Young

Published by: Demand Media Limited & G2 Entertainment Limited

Publishers: Jason Fenwick & Jules Gammond

Written by Liam McCann